ARCHITECTURAL DESIGN

UEST-EDITED BY
ARK TITMAN

THE NEW PASTORALISM
LANDSCAPE INTO ARCHITECTURE

03|2013

CHITECTURAL DESIGN
AY/JUNE 2013
SN 0003-8504

OFILE NO 223
BN 978-1118-336984

ARCHITECTURAL DESIGN

GUEST-EDITED BY
MARK TITMAN

THE NEW PASTORALISM: LANDSCAPE INTO ARCHITECTURE

106

PASTORALISM ALLOWS ARCHITECTURE
TO EXPLORE HUMAN-CENTRED
GREEN ISSUES THAT INTERPRET
AND COMMODIFY NATURE FOR THE
HIGHER AIM OF URBANITES' DELIGHT,
SELF- AND SPIRITUAL REALISATION.
— MARK TITMAN

60

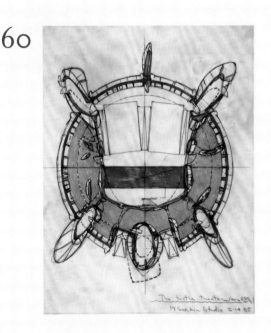

ARCHITECTURAL DESIGN

MAY/JUNE 2013
PROFILE NO 223

Editorial Offices
John Wiley & Sons
25 John Street
London WC1N 2BS
UK

T: +44 (0)20 8326 3800

Editor
Helen Castle

Managing Editor (Freelance)
Caroline Ellerby

Production Editor
Elizabeth Gongde

Prepress
Artmedia, London

Art Direction and Design
CHK Design:
Christian Küsters
Sophie Troppmair

Printed in Italy by Printer Trento Srl

Sponsorship/advertising
Faith Pidduck/Wayne Frost
T: +44 (0)1243 770254
E: fpidduck@wiley.co.uk

Subscribe to AD

AD is published bimonthly and is available to purchase on both a subscription basis and as individual volumes at the following prices.

Prices
Individual copies: £24.99/US$45
Individual issues on AD App
for iPad: £9.99/US$13.99
Mailing fees for print may apply

Annual Subscription Rates
Student: £75 / US$117 print only
Personal: £120 / US$189 print and iPad access
Institutional: £212 / US$398 print or online
Institutional: £244 / US$457 combined print and online
6-issue subscription on AD App for iPad: £44.99/US$64.99

Subscription Offices UK
John Wiley & Sons Ltd
Journals Administration Department
1 Oldlands Way, Bognor Regis
West Sussex, PO22 9SA, UK
T: +44 (0)1243 843 272
F: +44 (0)1243 843 232
E: cs-journals@wiley.co.uk

Print ISSN: 0003-8504
Online ISSN: 1554-2769

Prices are for six issues and include postage and handling charges. Individual-rate subscriptions must be paid by personal cheque or credit card. Individual-rate subscriptions may not be resold or used as library copies.

All prices are subject to change without notice.

Rights and Permissions
Requests to the Publisher should be addressed to:
Permissions Department
John Wiley & Sons Ltd
The Atrium
Southern Gate
Chichester
West Sussex PO19 8SQ
UK

F: +44 (0)1243 770 620
E: permreq@wiley.co.uk

Front cover: Drawing from *The Land of Scattered Seeds*, 2001, by John Puttick. © John Puttick

Inside front cover: Detail from John Puttick, *The Land of Scattered Seeds*, 2001. © John Puttick

EDITORIAL
Helen Castle

New Pastoralism celebrates a newfound conviviality in the city through landscape. Philosophically, this challenges the current status quo in architectural thinking. For years, architecture has sought to engage with the perceived authenticity of the urban condition by positively seeking out and meeting its grittiness with no amelioration. The pastoral, in contrast, is, as Guest-editor Mark Titman describes it in the introduction, all about 'comfortable and joyous ways to engage the city dweller with the delights of natural landscape' (p 14). New Pastoralism's aspiration for benevolent pleasure and mediation is reflected in pastoralism's resonance as a word. For the pastoral evokes not only the idealisation of the rural or the bucolic, but because of its associations with the caring shepherd's role in the New Testament, has a heritage that brings us the word 'pastor', and resurfaces in these more secular times in the ubiquitous use of 'pastoral care'.

The highly contemporary treatment of pastoralism advocated in this issue seeks a very ancient joy in the landscape through new media, technologies and expression. It is a very current tendency with a rich Western lineage, whether it is history paintings of scenes depicting Greek Arcadia or the very British tradition of William Blake and Samuel Palmer discovering Jerusalem in 'England's green and pleasant land' (pp 20–5); dramatically re-enacted for contemporary audiences in the Opening Ceremony of the London 2012 Olympic Games (see p 88). It is also one that has parallels with the Arabic or Moorish tradition of the cultivated garden as an urban haven, whether it is the Hanging Gardens of Babylon or those of the Alhambra. In this issue, traditions of East and West are most conspicuously assimilated in the work of Kathryn Findlay, who is not afraid to combine a very rustic British thatched roof in a building that is informed by the Japanese sensibility of Wabi-Sabi (see pp 32–9).

Can this pursuit of a new Arcadia, though, do anything more than provide architects with a quick-fix visionary release in these challenging times? Kevin Rhowbotham clearly thinks not in his scathing Counterpoint (pp 138–41); for him, it is a project that is clearly misguided by its Romantic impulses. What, however, is clear is that the subject of this issue proves a rich test bed for reimagining our relationship with nature – taking in speculative projects by the likes of Michael Sorkin, MVRDV, François Roche and Liam Young – and contesting the conventional polemic of the urban and the rural. ᴆ

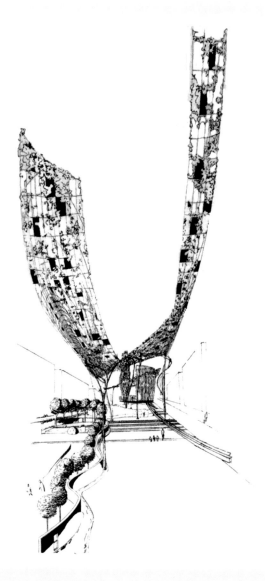

Mark Titman, *Rangers House*, Greenwich
Park, London, watercolour, 1994
top: Portrait of the copper beech tree under
which a couple were married, commissioned as
a memento for their travels abroad.

Mark Titman, *Solar Park*, Berlin, ink on
tracing paper, 1995
left: Photovoltaic cells line the ivy-and-grape
covered canopy that hovers over Potsdammer
Platz's 600-metre (1,968-feet) long inhabited
hedge.

Mark Titman, *Windswept*, Greenwich Park,
London, watercolour, 1999
above: Channelling a tribe of trees to distance
the critical eye revealed a complex park life of
wonderful colour and vibrancy that enveloped
the sitter.

Mark Titman, thinker, painter and director of the small Dorset-based architectural practice Titman Design, has undertaken 10 years of research into green architecture. During this time, as a senior lecturer at Greenwich University and while running Unit 22 at the Bartlett School of Architecture, University College London (UCL), with Jeremy Till, he and his students have explored the broadest notions of sustainability. He was tutored by Elia Zenghelis and Pascal Schöning before practising with John Miller, Trevor Horne and Richard Horden. His artwork includes printing and painting, in which he depicts the immersive sense of space that the countryside and parks can give their inhabitants. Many of his pieces are used to vitalise the spaces where they are hung. He uses various techniques including channelling, marbling, collage and watercolour washes to benefit from the intuitive and happenstance complexities of the media in order to convey the animate nature of such spaces.

Mark also established the GREENwich FORUM (www.greenwichforum.net/) to see what is happening in green architecture, science, art, literature and 'nature' that can better effect our views of the built environment and our relationship with the natural world.

He has exhibited his designs at the Design Centre, Building Centre, Stephen Lawrence Gallery, Bear Space and the Laban Centre, all in London, and has been published in international design magazines. He was previously a research fellow at the Royal College of Art (RCA) and a consultant to the European Space Agency, and has also worked with the Creatureshop animatronics company to prepare installations for the Design Council.

Titman Design's projects include housing developments and conversions which include an element of integrated planting and/or wildlife. The practice recently won the commission from Tiffany & Co to design drinking fountains for London's Royal Parks, the first of which is already installed in Green Park. Mark is currently working with a government task force looking at ways to set up a new model park that will influence the design of 200 new and existing parks across the UK. ᗡ

Mike Aling

Prounstretcher MCMXLII, After *Went The Day Well?*, 2012
An Internet shopping distribution centre doubles up as a cinema with communal spaces in a small village in the Chilterns, as depicted in Alberto Cavalcanti's *Went the Day Well?* (1942). A social condenser with a magnetic polymer envelope, rippling in unison with the signals of local virtual traffic.

Prounstretcher MMI, After *This Filthy Earth*, 2012
An augmented reality (non-religious) wedding venue in remote
Cumbria. Augmented reality can potentially alleviate the
increasing costs of wedding ceremonies and civil partnerships
in the UK. In this scheme, urbanites can wash in a digitally wet
augmented architecture that takes its precedent from director
Andrew Kotting's *This Filthy Earth* (2001) – a manically
grotesque, Bruegel-the-Elder-like cinematic interpretation of
Émile Zola's novel *La Terre* (1887).

Michael Tompert

12LVE [4] Targeting, 2010
Tompert finds intricate beauty in the precise destruction of an iPhone. The facets of the bullet's crater catch the light in a range of iridescent colours.

12LVE [4] *Book Burning,* **2010**
Several layers of an iPad are revealed with its burning. That the digital keyboard display persists under that carbon and fractured glass seems improbable.

Alastair Parvin

Server, Watford Gap, Northamptonshire, 2009
Shared knowledge and open data will themselves
be seen as renewable resources, fundamental to
constructing a better urban-rural citizenship.

M1
SERVER

Visitors	106.1FM
Children	106.5FM
Workers	106.2FM
Research	106.8FM

Mark Titman, *Albert Memorial and Emperor Butterfly*, digital collage, 2011
The vibrant wings elevate the gravitas of death through metaphor and association.

DUALISM IS DEAD; LONG LIVE THE PASTORAL

Croix de Waltham, restaurée.

We live in an age of environmental doom-saying, informational overload, greater lifestyle choices, shifting family structures and increasingly sedentary living patterns. Also, we live in a time of more competing ideas, conflicting offers that confuse our desires oppositional agendas and dichotomies that dilute our intentions. It is thus easy to perceive ourselves to be in between the close of an old era and on the brink of a new one. We are split and living in a time of dualities.

In his film *Dead Man* (1995), director Jim Jarmusch placed his half-dying character William Blake in a forest wilderness, where he walks through the midst of life and death, encountering a looseness of mind and human morals that forces him to confront his own true experience of life's hardships and wonders. This journey could just as easily have happened in the city or in an office, but neither he nor the audience can easily escape the forest's timeless continuum. Yet the audience can connect more profoundly with the forest than with the cities Jarmusch used in *Night On Earth* (1991). The very looseness of the forest, hills and shoreline give no restrictive cultural programme or practical agenda to react to, as the city does. The lack of human context forces William Blake to look inwards, terrified by lack of meaning, to search for something – only to finally be at peace before he dies.

This ancient wilderness of the mind and landscape has, over the millennia, attracted the attention of artists and writers as we have become urbanised and sense a lack of something within us in city life. Our sense of that loss of looseness, play and risk can be found in films like Claude Faraldo's *Themroc* (1973), Terry Gilliam's *Brazil* (1985) and John Boorman's *The Emerald Forest* (1985), and books such as JG Ballard's *High-Rise* (1975)[1] and Thomas Pynchon's *Gravity's Rainbow* (1973),[2] which all present reactions to the constrictions of urbanisation, and offer wilderness as an escape.

The escape we really tend to take, however, is not walks through the landscape, but the distraction of mental travels into alcohol, drugs and cyberspace in search of challenges we seem unable to find in our everyday lives. The environment, and possibly architecture, can help us embark on an alternative inward journey.

To journey in the context of landscape is to reconnect to a deeper part of ourselves, to not be connected with others and their ideas, but share a deeper sense of 'quale' that architecture negates in its need to secure, commodify and make accessible. The landscape, desert and forest somehow enhance, magnify and distort the human condition, its very complexity echoing our inner life. English novelist John Fowles, in *The Tree* (1979), likens the forest to our brains, a sort of extended mind where we can hide from the linear thinking of cities and reconnect to our Green Man within: he suggests cities should be more like forests.[3] I suggest that architects rediscover the psychological and spiritual benefits of forests, mountains, caves, lagoons, beaches and dells in our attempts at urban planning and architecture.

Louis Kahn called such essential places the conceptual 'laws', upon which the architect could then set about 'designing', without which, he argued, the rules of design were wasted.[4] How often have you seen 'designed' architecture and not made any connection with the space? Yet the urge to comprehend and connect with the landscape or use it as a backdrop has possessed Western culture for centuries. Our architecture, from the classic.

iano rustico and Frank Lloyd Wright's 'land-huggers', to
he 'sky hooks' of the Constructivists and skyscrapers of New
ork, all have elemental references. Perhaps now such natural
eferences could be more intimate and subtle.

piritual Sustainability Versus Green Monoculture

he pastoral is just such an elemental type. It allows a
onnection of opposites, it is a harmony of dualities, is gentle and
orgiving, and a comfortable and joyous way to engage the city
weller with the delights of natural landscape. In this issue of
D it is shown as a mediator of polarities, including city:country,
igh-tech:low-tech, body:machine, rational:romantic,
icro:macro, inside:outside. The pastoral can balance seemingly
onflicting opposites whose traditional division and disunion
ow require balance and reunion. It is set in the context of
ythic harmony in reaction to the purely utilitarian approach
reen architects often adopt and have promoted since the 1960s
hen environmentalism became popular. Then, Austrian painter
nd self-confessed dirt artist Friedensreich Hundertwasser noted
at many environmentalists were losing a sense of beauty and
omplexity, and the ability to respond to earth, giving way to
echanical sustainability devoid of human engagement.[5] Here,
eoff Ward continues this theme of the benefits of dirt with a
iological look at environmentalism (pp 82–5), while Nic Clear
emonstrates the pastoral role in his research into modern myths
nd sci-fi backdrops to contemporary narratives (pp 86–93).

This distinction between the mechanical and the organic
ighlights the contrast between concern and care. While much
reen architecture, though concerned, is driven by ecological
ar and consumer guilt, a pastoral architecture cares, in that it
gentle, generous, and yet able to incorporate much energy-
ving high-tech. Being open-ended and not solely mechanically
irected, it can encompass a variety of conflicting elements.

In 1992, while consulting the European Space Agency
on efficient ways of making space stations habitable, I studied
payloads, volumetrics, ergonomics, train, car and aircraft
interiors, but quickly found, when a particular group of
astronauts threatened to strike, that space stations should be,
more importantly, hospitable. At this point we stopped pure
scientific research of access, storage and facilities planning
diagrams and began to consider the space station as a potential
place of ease, familiarity and comfort. Barbarella, holiday
resorts and the old country cottage became considerations
for keeping the valuable astronauts happy: even an inglenook
fireplace became feasible. Most interestingly, the artificial
growth of plants became important not only for food, oxygen
and biochemical experiments, but for the pleasure of the
inhabitants, the efficiency of 1960s high-tech becoming linked
with the simple low-tech delights of yore. Examples of this can
be seen in Kathryn Findlay's thatched high-tech pool houses
(see pp 32–9) and John Puttick's communal garden designs in
Land of Scattered Seeds (pp 40–47).

Vitruvius's three fundamental precepts of firmness,
commodity and delight[6] can now all be linked, suggesting that
architecture need not neglect pleasure. In particular the human
love of nature is back in the equation: it is architecturally
efficient to create delight. But inevitably it is an increasingly
artificial sort of nature, now that every tree in England exists
on a map, and the farmer knows where to fertilise his fields via
satellite. The efficiency of high-tech monitoring of processes
in farming and animal welfare are explored in this issue in
Alastair Parvin's meticulous analysed and responsive Server
project (pp 118–25) and in Matthew Cannon and Mascia
Gianvanni's inclusion of a menagerie in London's Canary
Wharf (pp 68–73).

he landscape, desert and
orest somehow enhance,
nagnify and distort the human
ondition, its very complexity
choing our inner life.

Section A

rek Draper, Book Shop, Oxford Street,
ndon, 2009
ndered section. A sequence of browsing
aces lead the book seeker in, through and
und various reading nooks and interior
enery to slow the busy shopper.

Stefano Boeri, Bosco Verticale, Milan, 2011
The dense acres of forest that once graced the countryside have been pulled
vertically and sit regally illuminating a small footprint in the grey city.

Myth and Delight

In today's increasingly virtual environments, Vitruvius's delight
seems to have become less physically relevant, yet we need
physical delight and natural engagement more than ever to help
balance body and mind. The facade in architecture has become
too important; the slick surface detailing of Renzo Piano's
glass 'Shard' (2012) and Foster + Partners' slippery smooth
'Gherkin' (2004) in London reveal a mechanical animosity. In
ancient times we would have been able to delve, move, touch
and pass through surfaces, but these seem to reflect and reject
us. Originally it was our physically interactive interface with
our landscapes that inspired us to make spaces and evolve
tools and minds; simply put, our physical capacity to play with
environments led to our brain development. Today this interface
is becoming invisible, reducing our capacity to interact with
physical spaces or objects, and thus to think and evolve through
immersive play.

Putting landscape back into architecture in a pastoral
way would allow us to do this, as touched upon in Dominic
Shepherd's social understanding of Lucas Cranach the Elder's
painting *The Golden Age* (c 1530) (see pp 26–31), and more
directly in MVRDV's creation of a planted coastal hotel
development in Galije, Montenegro (pp 48–55). Contrasting
narratives, contexts and characters can be unified in the dialectics
of the pastoral. Designing with dialectics, dual interpretations

and multiple narratives that can coexist ambiguously offers a
richer, more multilayered architecture. Elements of landscape
and building, city and country, practical and poetic, Classical and
Gothic, West and East, high- and low-tech, biomech, spiritual-
material, left-right, can be combined under a single umbrella.
Today architecture's objectives are increasingly complex, but
the pastoral offers an enjoyable way to combine and intuitively
interpret or ignore opposing aspects of urban living and
contemporary systems.

Since we began moving to cities, we have compensated for
our loss of connection with nature by engaging in vicarious
leisure substitutes. This desire still exists, as demonstrated by its
frequent use in the propaganda of green politics, conservation
and lifestyle advertising, and increasingly in films such as those
cited in Mike Aling's 'Digital Cottage Industries' article on pp
100–105. Yet in the past it was the context for most poetry,
literature and art, in all cultures: Claude Lévi-Strauss points out
that this ongoing longing is hard-wired into us, making us happy
to accept the artificial substitutes of culture.[7]

So if the social imperative is to create buildings that are
both physically engaging and emotionally uplifting and sociable,
what form could they take? As the modern urbanite becomes
increasingly isolated, immersed in data and remote from nature,
could an element of wilderness prevent him from becoming

Mark Titman, Robin Monotti and James Furzer, Watering Holes, Green Park, London, 2010
A 3-D rendering of the drinking fountain with holes for adults, children, wheelchair users and dogs offers a timeless reconnection to drinking, the earth and sky.

In today's increasingly virtual environments, Vitruvius's delight seems to have become less physically relevant, yet we need physical delight and natural engagement more than ever to help balance body and mind.

characterless? Can the literary notions of negation, contradiction and narrative, used by the pastoralists Virgil, John Milton, William Blake, Edmund Spenser and William Shakespeare be used to engage an urban audience in physical space? The pastoral wilderness, a place of endless copulation, growth and death, both fearsome and invigorating, intrigues and engages us, yet at the same time negates us. It can bring us back into the now by being risky, by allegorising, and attracting us all into the dialogue by inverting the urban narrative. The devices used in Spenser's *The Faerie Queene* (1590–96) and Milton's *Paradise Lost* (1667) can be made architectural.

Animate Architecture

The subliminal influences of natural environments on the individual define the setting of the personal experience, and are highly influenced by an active living element. Look at the Samuel Palmer imagery of the sublime that Colin Harrison presents in this issue (pp 20–25). Consider experiences such as reading on a park bench under a tree with a bird singing in it, sitting on a window seat in the kitchen in winter stroking a cat, smoking in a summer courtyard with a water feature and swimming carp at your side. The human, animal or natural elements used to create such multilayered spaces are buildable, yet alive and not entirely controlled. They are messy because they incorporate human experience, other life forms and empathy. How can all this otherness be distilled into a building?

Plants and creatures were humanity's first connection with 'other' life, allowing displaced understandings of human relationships and activities to be played out. Most of our deep cultural memories, dreams and archetypal stories include mythic battles, loves, deaths, betrayals, alliances and so on, with creatures interacting with each other or humans. Heraldry, totems, mascots, mythical creatures and logos stem from these interactions. What if companies and households were to seek to express themselves through their architecture more emotively and engagingly using animals (living or abstract) and living nature? What if architects inspired communities to reveal the

Suzanne Moxhay, *Eventide*, digital collage, 2012
The city rests in timeless inhabitation and distant buzz.

strengths of today's tribes, such as those of a hungry lion, a sleeping gazelle or a snapping crocodile? A lion space would empower a neighbourhood, revitalise a street, energise a square, and once again bring individuals face to face to articulate desire, courage and hope in real time and space – not simply via a Facebook photo or Tweet. A personal and tribal expression would be shared and emotional; to give an expressive and empowering architecture that both suits a specific group of urban dwellers and tells them: 'This is not neutral reflective surface; this is a live space.'

Proverb: 'Out of strength comes forth sweetness.'

The characters, legends and powerful dynamics of a chosen creature have offered tribes, clans, armies, nations and teams inspiration and security, an expression of their social identity and focus for their rituals. The forms of buildings today are often abstract, lacking not only meaning, but also any coherent visual composition or articulation. Consider Zaha Hadid, Frank Gehry and the parametric architects. Now consider how animals could help form an architecture of some significance and social dynamic.

Out of strength comes forth sweetness.

Proverb: 'All creatures say their names.'

In the Pig Restaurant, or Grasshopper Yoghurt Bar, the biology of the creature offers coded meaning and biomimetic design opportunities; the fat body, the springy legs. Michael Sorkin has developed projects such as his Animal Houses, Herd Houses, Turtle Portable Theatre and Starfish Revolving Restaurant over the past two decades (see pp 60–67). The adaptive behaviours that natural creatures display provide critical knowledge for the design of ecologically responsive and sustainable systems, as well as suggesting new forms of engaging architecture. Consider: a firefly's synchronous light-pulse dances, whale song, the bioluminescent angler fish – our understanding of their behaviour can inspire intelligent eco-environments and buildings that communicate and interact with each other and the world around them. Can architecture do this? This is explored by François Roche in R&Sie(n)/New Territories' An Architecture 'des humeurs' research project (see pp 126–33).

But where can we look to place such buildings? What of the urban planning scale? The dells, hills, desert, seashore and the forests mentioned earlier are humanity's deep landscapes of the psyche, places both understood and yet mysterious. The best myths and fables are located in a version of these pastoral archetypes, which are also embedded in us and in the village, city and nation. The UK government is now starting to place value on this, by comparing various scenic landscapes and giving them corresponding notional monetary indicators linked to tourism, health and leisure metrics. But how does one put value in monetary and accountable ways on such spiritual, living and emotive aspects of a New Jerusalem?

Mark Titman, *Snake Bridge*, oil on card, 2000
A flexing bridge that offers wildlife a *safe* crossing adapts to tidal levels and raises itself using water ballast to bend like a fishing rod.

To give conclusive urban value to animals (living or abstract) and planting in our cities would require an index by which each building footprint has a metric 'life rating' of species originally present on the site, to indicate what equivalent species or abstraction should inhabit the completed building by way of replacement. Planning strategies and laws could enforce the inclusion of new species to replace the displaced; to ensure that developments do not ultimately detract from the biosphere, but actually enhance it. This index would allow spaces of nature to become commodities that the economic and mechanical aspects of society would have to respect and learn to appreciate, rather than simply wipe out. After all, isn't saving the planet a lot about saving the life of the earth – or better still, improving it?

Towards a New Jerusalem

Now that the zero-carbon house and energy-efficient architecture of the 1990s have been achieved, green architecture can aspire to more. Pastoralism allows architects to explore human-centred green issues that interpret and commodify nature for the higher aim of urbanites' delight, self- and spiritual realisation. In the future, each time we build we could use the abovementioned index to convert from being designers to being the playful custodians; to enhance the liveliness of a building and city. The emerging Jerusalem requires architects to re-evaluate themselves, and to see sustainability as a means of heightening spiritual, mental and social wellbeing as well as our physical needs.

The cultural meme of a pastoral Eden or Arcadia is ancient, yet has an ongoing reality reinforced by each generation due to its timeless universal nature. Ironically, the romantic allure of the pastoral is used today to sell predominantly inorganic and technological environments as architects, politicians and planners offer city dwellers visions of utopian spaces by enhancing the products' 'green appeal', thus gaining our acceptance of cold architecture and invisible communications. But the dream of the pastoral cannot be so easily satisfied. Its dramatic yet practical and optimistic fantasy, which single-minded Modernism and its clean, empty heart has ignored, is much needed today to counteract our increasing isolation and powerlessness in a doom-laden and cynical world.

We all know country life had, and has, its hardships, which is why so many of us live in cities, but the pastoral myth remains, to gratify urban nostalgia and give us hope and a connection to something missing. Such ancient pastoral hints, and those more contemporary ones you will find in this issue, give architects a structure and optimis that need not make sense, but is self-evident, joyful and helpful in our times of massive change and insecurity – an opportunity to build the Jerusalem we all think we remember. ⌂

Notes
JG Ballard, *High-Rise*, Jonathon Cape (London), 1975.
Thomas Pynchon, *Gravity's Rainbow*, Penguin Books (London), 1973.
John Fowles, *The Tree*, Little Brown (London), 1979.
Robert Charles Twombly, *Louis Kahn: Essential Texts*, WW Norton and Co (New York), 2003.
Harry Rand, *Hundertwasser*, Taschen (Cologne), 1991.
See Morris Hicky Morgan, *Vitruvius: The Ten Books Of Architecture*, Harvard University Press, Humphrey Milford and Oxford University Press (Cambridge, MA, London and Oxford), 1914.
Claude Lévi-Strauss, *Myth and Meaning: Cracking the Code of Culture*, University of Toronto Press (Toronto), 1978.

Michael Krinou, Aviary and Dovecote, Deptford High Street, London, 2010
Zoomorphic forms are given strength when the millennia-evolved camouflage is applied to a dovecote.

Samuel Palmer, Leaf from a sketchbook, pen and brown ink, *c* 1824–5
The leaves from Palmer's most important surviving sketchbook include many ideas for visionary landscapes that were never executed. Here, a pilgrim passes a biblical herdsman, perhaps Job, and his flock.

SAMUEL PALMER

AND THE

PASTORAL VISION

Colin Harrison, Senior Curator of European Art at the Ashmolean Museum in Oxford, describes how the English 19th-century artist Samuel Palmer was deeply influenced by the poet and painter William Blake. Palmer's sublime paintings of the 1820s placed a new emphasis on the harmony of nature, reinterpreting traditional subjects entirely afresh, placing the Holy Family not in the Holy Land, but in the English countryside.

one of his minor works, the preface to *Milton: a* *em* (1804–10), the English poet and artist William ake (1757–1827) created a vivid contrast between the ngland of the Industrial Revolution, exemplified the 'dark Satanic Mills', and the England of the cond Coming of Christ, a land of 'mountains green', easant pastures', and 'clouded hills':

I will not cease from Mental Fight,
Nor shall my Sword sleep in my hand:
Till we have built Jerusalem,
In England's green & pleasant Land.

espite these visions of a 'green and pleasant land', ndscape played only a minor role in Blake's own ctures. It was left to his most eminent disciple, muel Palmer (1805–81), to illustrate Blake's ideal. Palmer's education was essentially literary. His her was a bookseller, and he was taught at home by s nurse, Mary Ward, a simple woman whom Palmer

described in later life as being 'ripe in that without which so much is often useless or mischievous: deeply read in her bible and *Paradise Lost*.'[1] Among his favourite authors were the standard classics such as Shakespeare, Chaucer and Spenser, but he reserved a special place for John Milton (1608–74): he was able to recite long passages of *Paradise Lost* from memory, and greatly admired the early poems – *Lycidas*, *Comus*, *L'Allegro*, and *Il Penseroso*. He found 'all my dearest landscape longings embodied' in the Jacobean playwright John Fletcher's *Faithful Shepherdess* (1608–9).[2] His artistic education was deeply conventional, until 1824 when fellow English landscape painter John Linnell introduced him to Blake. It was not the grand Dante illustrations on which Blake was working that impressed Palmer, but the earlier illustrations for a schoolboy's edition of Virgil's *Eclogues*, 'visions of little dells, and nooks, and corners of Paradise; models of the exquisitest pitch of intense poetry'.[3]

The effect on Palmer's art was immediate. The sketchbook he began in 1824 is full of intensely individual studies of landscapes, figures and animals drawn with no consideration for conventional proportion or perspective. The earliest mature painting by Palmer depends on these studies: the *Repose of the Holy Family* (c 1824–5) was painted in the technique that Blake had called 'tempera', incorporating quotations from Blake and Albrecht Dürer (1471–1528), and this most traditional of subjects was reinterpreted in a wholly new way: for the Holy Family is placed, not in Egypt, but in the English countryside, specifically in the Darent Valley near Shoreham in Kent.

Palmer followed this early work with some of his greatest masterpieces, in which his vision of the English landscape is seen at its most intense. The six drawings in sepia ink made in 1825 exemplify his originality. The technique, of ink mixed with thick gum to give the appearance of the chiaroscuro woodcut, was wholly new, and never repeated. His imagery, although ostensibly literary – there are quotations from Virgil, Chaucer, Shakespeare and other authors attached to all these landscapes – derives from a close study of Old Master prints, from Blake, and from an intense examination of the countryside around Shoreham.

All these landscapes show man in completely harmonious communion with nature under the watchful tutelage of the Anglican church. For, as Palmer noted:

> Landscape is of little value, but as it hints or expresses the haunts or doings of man. However gorgeous, it can be but Paradise without an Adam. Take away its churches, where for centuries the pure word of God has been read to the poor … and you have a frightful kind of Paradise left – a Paradise without a God.[4]

The drawing that perhaps epitomises Palmer's vision is *The Valley thick with Corn* (1825), which evokes lines from Psalm 65: 'Thou crownest the year with thy goodness; and thy paths drop fatness … and the little hills shall rejoice on every side.' For, although essentially Christian, Palmer's vision combines the abundance of God's bounty with a neo-Platonic interpretation of man's relationship with nature.

With the encouragement of Linnell, later to become his father-in-law, Palmer applied his visionary style to more ostensibly literal studies from nature. Despite his determination 'never [to] be a naturalist by profession',[5] Palmer produced some of his most memorable images by drawing in front of the motif. They were always imbued with religion and emotion, and the best of them has something supernatural, an intensity of observation and feeling far beyond Linnell's prescription. Even in these drawings, Palmer associated external nature with descriptions he had found in his reading. Unlike the drawings made in emulation of the Old Masters, these nature studies have an extraordinary chromatic range, from brilliant orange to fuliginous black.

Parallel with his experiments with high colour, Palmer continued to explore the possibilities of monochrome, exhibiting a group of what he referred to as 'blacks' at the Royal Academy of Arts, London, in 1832. The subjects were often the shepherds and sheep described in Virgil's *Eclogues*, but the style was still indebted to Blake. Gradually, however, Palmer's youthful self-confidence waned, worldly cares preoccupied him, and he began to heed Linnell's advice to prefer naturalism over imagination. In 1835, he left Shoreham for good, and it was not until the 1860s that he resumed his most visionary style. By this date, he was married, had lost two children, and had settled in Redhill, a busy railway junction in Surrey, where he 'read, or drew, or dreamt of the past'.

William Blake, *Thenot and Colinet*, wood engraving for RJ Thornton's *Pastorals of Virgil*, London, 1821

opposite top: Although Blake's illustrations were modest in scale and ambition, they were among his few landscapes, and had an enormous influence on Palmer and other young artists.

Landscape is of little value, but as it hints or expresses the haunts or doings of man. However gorgeous, it can be but Paradise without an Adam. Take away its churches, where for centuries the pure word of God has been read to the poor … and you have a frightful kind of Paradise left – a Paradise without a God.

Samuel Palmer, *Landscape with the Repose of the Holy Family*, oil and tempera and pen and ink on panel, *c* 1824–5
above bottom: This traditional subject is firmly placed in the Kent countryside – a preliminary drawing records that the hillside is based on Shoreham Paddock.

Samuel Palmer, *The Valley thick with Corn*, pen and brush in dark brown ink mixed with gum, varnished, 1825
The motif of a reader in a landscape is traditional in English art, and is here placed in the countryside of the Darent Valley near Shoreham in Kent.

Samuel Palmer, *Early Morning*, pen and brush in dark brown ink mixed with gum, varnished, 1825
The group of harvesters nestling in the fold of the hill epitomises man's harmony with nature, their home on the horizon.

Samuel Palmer, *Shepherds under a Full Moon*, pen and brown ink, brush in Indian ink, with bodycolour and gum, c 1829–30
Although it is indebted to Blake's illustrations to Virgil, Palmer's monochrome introduces a mystic quality that is wholly original.

Palmer's last years were taken up with two main projects: the completion of his translation of Virgil's *Eclogues*, and the production of a series of eight large watercolours illustrating Milton's *L'Allegro* and *Il Penseroso*. The watercolours, and the etchings derived from them, marked a return to the visionary landscapes of the Shoreham period. In *The Lonely Tower* (1879), the most personal of these works, Palmer strove for 'poetic loneliness';[6] while he described *The Bellman*, of the same year, as 'a breaking out of village-fever long after contact – a dream of that genuine village where I mused away some of my best years, designing what nobody would care for, and contracting, among good books, a fastidious and unpopular taste.'[7] ⌷

Gradually, however, Palmer's youthful self-confidence waned, worldly cares preoccupied him, and he began to heed Linnell's advice to prefer naturalism over imagination.

NOTES

1. Raymond Lister (ed), *The Letters of Samuel Palmer*, Clarendon Press (Oxford), 1974, p 823.
2. Ibid, p 1012.
3. AH Palmer, *The Life and Letters of Samuel Palmer, Painter and Etcher*, Seeley & Co. (London), 1892, p 15.
4. *The Letters of Samuel Palmer*, op cit, p 516.
5. Ibid, p 36.
6. Ibid, p 695.
7. Ibid, p 970.

Samuel Palmer, *Oak Tree and Beech, Lullingstone Park*, pencil, pen and brown ink, and watercolour, heightened with gouache, and gum arabic, on grey paper, 1828
In a letter, Palmer wrote that 'Milton by one epithet, draws an oak of the largest girth I ever saw; "Pine and *Monumental* Oak"; I have just been trying to draw a large one in Lullingstone; but the poet's tree is huger than anything in the park.'

Dominic Shepherd

THE GOLDEN AGE

BETWEEN WILDERNESS AND UTOPIA

WHAT IF EDEN IN FACT IS STILL ALL AROUND US?

WHAT IF WE NEVER LEFT IT AFTER ALL, THE ONLY DIFFERENCE BEING THAT GOD WITHDREW FROM THE PICTURE, LEAVING US ALONE WITH OUR OWN DISCONTENTS?

IN THAT CASE WE CAN EITHER, IN GOD'S ABSENCE, KEEP THE GARDEN OR DESTROY IT.

— ROBERT POGUE HARRISON, *GARDENS: AN ESSAY ON THE HUMAN CONDITION*, 2008[1]

Artist **Dominic Shepherd** pursues the imaginative and a sense of mystery in his work; his 2012 one-man show at Charlie Smith London was entitled 'Jerusalem'. Here he reflects on the Golden Age as depicted in Cranach's masterpiece of that name, and ruminates on the cyclical nature of the pastoral, a landscape that is tended and nurtured by generations of hands.

In the Alte Pinakothek in Munich, a city surrounded by the Bavarian forest, resides a painting by Lucas Cranach the Elder (1472–1553) titled *The Golden Age* (*c* 1530). Here, naked figures transport themselves in a garden redolent of Eden; a single tree acts as a maypole around which the folk gambol naked; the lion lies down with the fawn; the vines are heavy, fru and flowers abound. A high brick wall keeps them safe from the world beyond, where castles perched on cliff tops speak of external strife and politics. The concept of the Golden Age derives from Greek mythology, the first of five ages of man, where he lives in harmony with nature and his surroundings. When Cranach created this work at the beginning of the 16th century, the world, and our perception of it, was changing; the renaissance view (that drew on classical Greek thought) of the universe was replacing the medieval. There is no God floating in the sky; this is man and woman on their earthly patch.

There are walls, actually fences, around the annual Glastonbury festival in the West Country of England. The festival takes its name from the nearby town and Tor, which are associated with King Arthur, the Holy Grail and Joseph of Arimathea, acting as a nexus of myth and nationhood. Here the English tribes revisit their spiritual homeland at midsummer to dance and gambol naked of their more mundane urban lives. The folk revival of the mid-20th century gave birth to the Summer of Love generation, one attempt to get our selves back to the Garden. The original free festivals of this period, such as Stonehenge, could be seen as latter-day attempts to re-create the Epicurean garden schools, imploding under hedonistic excess and the bitterness of political strife.

Lucas Cranach the Elder, *The Golden Age***, oil on panel,** *c* **1530**
previous spread: Set in the first of Hesiod's five ages of human existence on earth, peace reigns as man and woman live together in harmony with nature.

Dominic Shepherd, *The Family***, oil on canvas, 2012**
above: The collapse of linear time that brought about paintings like "The Family" allows encounters between Guy Fawkes and the Incredible String Band, Romantic poets and Morris Dancers, witches and hippies, William Blake and Pearly Kings and Queens, the New Model Army and the radical movements of the sixties, and, well, Levellers and the Levellers, at a metaphorical banquet or feast'. Gavin Parkinson, 'Festival, or, First and Last of England', an article written to accompany Dominic Shepherd's exhibition 'Jerusalem' at Charlie Smith, London, 2012.

Dominic Shepherd, *New Jerusalem***, oil on canvas, 2012**
'What is now proved was once, only imagin'd.'
William Blake, *The Marriage of Heaven and Hell, c* 1790.

In Cranach's garden, all are naked, there is no hierarchy
of uniform or dress, no Marie Antoinette playing dairymaid.
The music festivals of summer echo this equality; the flimsy
tents, the basic latrines, the adverse weather, all suffer the
privations. With the advent of increasingly expensive tickets,
VIP areas, barbed wire and fences, this levelling is in danger
of evaporating, bringing hierarchy to the fields, where the rich
disport themselves in the garden created by the poor. Are
the revellers in Cranach's tableau destined to become the
idle aristocrats of the erotic gardens by Jean-Antoine Watteau
(1684–1721), or rather the precursors to the ideals of William
Blake (1757–1827), 'Levellers' reclaiming their land to till,
dancing within the New Jerusalem they have nurtured?

When travelling through the West Country, through the
chequerboard of fields and copses, I am reminded that the
garden of England was created by hundreds of hands going
back generations that nurtured and defined these spaces. The
pastoral is not wilderness where wolves roam, nor is it the
tyrannical straight lines of agribusiness. What defines these
spaces is care; pastoral care requires constant upkeep, the
sense that you might have to put more in than you receive.
If you lie in the sun, the weeds will grow. The garden reflects
our own fragile nature, the walls can crumble; we can be cast
out of Eden. In Cranach's painting, the tree is pollarded, and
somebody's hand pruned and trained the vines.

In the National Gallery in London is the companion piece
to The Golden Age, Lucas Cranach's The Close of the Silver
Age (c 1530). The garden gone, wilderness presses close.
Men fight and kill each other over the women who bear their
children. Mistrust, acquisitiveness and ownership have broken
the communality and custodianship of the garden, hierarchies
are forming, progress is being made. There is no vision for the
future, satisfaction with the present or affirmation of the past,
just a frenzy of inarticulate action as the divided peoples are
faced with an inevitable demise. Let us turn from this image of
closure to consider how we reaffirm our place in the continuum
and garden of ourselves.

Reflecting the ring of 'maypole' dancers in the former
painting, hands joined in a continuous link, pastoral space
is cyclical rather than progressive. It is defined diurnally and
by seasons, encompassing the repetitive custodial benefits
of pastoral care. 'Folk' or 'folklore' are forms of how we
engage with cyclical time; culture is passed down through the
generations in oral, artefact or ritual form, creating connections
to the past, establishing familial and locational ties. This form of
articulation is constantly enacted in the yearly cycle of festivities
and ritual, whether in religious and cultural celebrations of
rebirth in spring or on the football terraces where tribal loyalties
and heraldic colours are displayed.

*There is no vision for the future, satisfaction
with the present or affirmation of the past,
just a frenzy of inarticulate action as the
divided peoples are faced with an inevitable
demise.*

**Lucas Cranach the Elder, *The Close of
the Silver Age*, oil on oak, c 1530**
left: Set in the era following the Golden Age,
it falls apart as a tangle of quarrelsome
figures fight within a wild and uncouth
landscape.

**Dominic Shepherd, *Oracles*, oil on
canvas, 2012**
right: Pearly Kings and Queens are a
living part of urban folk in London, walking
artefacts with their insignia and lucky
charms stitched in pearly buttons.

Built into the act of the ritual is the stilling of time, a stepping outside of the daily routine to stop and reflect. In Cranach's garden, every blade of grass, every leaf and flower is painstakingly realised. Seeing takes time, you have to dwell in this garden and give yourself to the contemplation of its minutiae. In *The Tree* (1979), English novelist John Fowles, whi walking in Whistman's Wood on Dartmoor, 'gardened by what man has introduced', uses nature's space for mental reflection contemplation and meander, forming a connection between the twisting branches of the trees and his own neural links.[2] By holding nature up as a sublime mirror, he breaks from Cartesia dualism and creates a bridge between his own and the tree's reality. The forest allows Fowles to formulate and construct ne types of complex space; internal mind and external stimuli are linked.

How do we define this pastoral space in contemporary terms? Where does it lie? Is it found in National Trust-preserved grounds or the empty fields of corn? Can one contemplate the idyllic when one has been told what to look at, and how to look at it? In Paul Farley and Michael Symmons Roberts's book *Edgelands* (2011),[3] the two wordsmiths wander the Northwest of England, finding resonances and poetic contemplation in the forgotten zones: landfill sites, business parks or railway sidings Surely these are not pastoral spaces, nobody 'cares' for them, yet it is the poet's eye that acts as the gardener, growing new forms of engagement with these spaces. These overlooked enclaves have, by common standards, a lacklustre physical presence, but the poets, like William Wordsworth roaming the Cumbrian mountains, give them mythical status. A close analog

would be Andrei Tarkovsky's seminal film *Stalker* (1979), where an artist and scientist enter a closed zone, the film moving from black and white to colour as they penetrate this 'edgelands' space. The zone acts as a 'Whistman's Wood' where we, the observers, join the quest. The director, in his attention to visual minutiae, acts as a gardener, tenderly leading the viewer to poetic epiphany. The gardener, the director, the architect; all construct their inner worlds, and the sacred emerges into the profane through the constructions of their minds.

Cranach's painting is not a representation of reality, but a product of his imagination. *The Golden Age*, like the garden it depicts, has been nurtured, in all its exacting detail, into being. Certain details – the hairstyles and architecture – set this idyll within Cranach's time period, although its title refers explicitly to a 'historical' precedent. Could it be that he was not nostalgically looking to the past, but constructing a vision for the present, a focus for the souls of his contemporaries? The Golden Age is an ideal that lives within us, but does not define us. It is within our imagination that one sees the invisible, the unformed, the possible. It is here, in the garden of the mind, that one can mentally construct and bring to bud the 'pastoral' for our present and future age. ∆

Notes
1. Robert Pogue Harrison, *Gardens: An Essay on the Human Condition*, University of Chicago Press (Chicago, IL), 2008, p 176.
2. John Fowles, *The Tree*, Little Brown (London),1979, p 53.
3. Paul Farley and Michael Symmons Roberts, *Edgelands: Journeys into England's True Wilderness*, Jonathan Cape (London), 2011.

THE GOLDEN AGE IS AN IDEAL THAT LIVES WITHIN US, BUT DOES NOT DEFINE US.

IT IS WITHIN OUR IMAGINATION THAT ONE SEES THE INVISIBLE, THE UNFORMED, THE POSSIBLE.

IT IS HERE, IN THE GARDEN OF THE MIND, THAT ONE CAN MENTALLY CONSTRUCT AND BRING TO BUD THE 'PASTORAL' FOR OUR PRESENT AND FUTURE AGE.

Dominic Shepherd, *The Tunnel*, digital photograph, 2011
Close to the springhead, a sinuous rill passes under the A35, a trunk road that winds its way through the West Country of England.

Dominic Shepherd, *The Puddle*, digital photograph, 2011
Reflection, surface and depth, a black mirror for our time.

Mark Titman

Ushida Findlay Architects, Soft and Hairy House, Tokyo, Japan, 1994
below and opposite: Located on a greenfield site, the design was guided by the clients'
interest in Salvador Dalí. They were particularly inspired by his statement that future
architecture would be 'soft and hairy'. As a result, the building harbours the unexpected
– where the architecture moves between dream and reality.

'YOU CAN TOUCH BUT DO NOT READ'

THE 'FUTURE-RUSTIC' WORK OF KATHRYN FINDLAY

By turns curvaceous, fluffy, leafy, green, soft and hairy', the work of **Kathryn Findlay** is palpably 'future-rustic' in all its formal and material manifestations. Guest-editor **Mark Titman** explains how Findlay's designs also more subtly respond 'to the richness of a given situation, the resources and natural conditions that each site and its surrounding context reveals', coming out of an approach that has been equally influenced by her rural childhood on a farm in Scotland as almost two decades of working in Japan.

Kathryn Findlay is an architect, cook and an accomplished speaker, who talks without the aid of a script or even written notes. The principal of Ushida Findlay Architects, she founded the practice in 1986 in Tokyo with her then partner Eisaku Ushida. In 1999 the studio returned to the UK – to Edinburgh. Since 2004, she has been leading the practice independently from London. Through her work, Findlay promotes a generous treatment of space and construction that integrates the use of traditional natural and even living materials with contemporary high-tech materials and technologies. Peter Cook has described her work as 'digi-thatch'.[1] Others have called it 'future-rustic'.[2] But, her architecture mostly responds to the richness of a given situation, the resources and natural conditions that each site and its surrounding context reveals and offers up to her. There is no fixed agenda with her work or any singular approach to design, which makes for a richer, more original type of green architecture.

The drawings show the frame of the city from which one can re-imagine the sky – so often obscured on urban walks by our looking downwards at asphalt, paving and enclosing buildings.

Kathryn's work is by turns curvaceous, fluffy, leafy, green, soft and hairy. It suggests a new material aesthetic where sensuousness and tactility create a timeless experience for engaging and dwelling in buildings, responding to the physicality of occupants' bodies. The rough simplicity of the Japanese concept of Wabi-Sabi – serenity and austerity – is invoked by her to provide a dualism of imperfect perfection. She uses multiple contrasting materials and contextual themes to create a depth and character that is most apparent on the surfaces of her buildings. These can be touched and inhabited, but they do not need to be read. These multiple experiences of the surroundings, when taken with the physical readings, offer a richer, deeper actuality.

At the forefront of an architecture that is both sensuous and luxurious – the senses being indulged through the use of living materials – Kathryn Findlay's designs do not conform to a conventional understanding of green architecture. This is not mere greenery for greenery's sake – nor ubiquitous surface planting – but of sensual enhancement, material pleasure and intimate touch. This is not ostentatious luxury. Here is an architecture that invokes for its inhabitants a joyful sensory abundance and physical delight. It is neither withdrawn nor cold. Its complex forms are not generated from abstraction, but of measured and heartfelt responses to the sun, circulation, site and contextual expressions.

When Ushida Findlay designed one of the first vertical gardens in 1999 for the Gorbals Police Station in Glasgow to be reclad in a tartan checked pattern of heather and green planting in swivel panels, the firm's attention to contextual layering brought forth a character that is both lively yet intentionally gentle. This is an essential vitality that is not slavish to trends or perceived necessity. The need to contextualise and bring life to an urban area necessitated the inclusion of planting as a universally acceptable medium, yet the tartan also localised this.

Ushida Findlay Architects, Doha Art Foundation and Official Residence, Doha, Qatar, 2002–
top: This art foundation and VIP guest reception was commissioned by the Minister of Culture and National Heritage who wanted a building similar to the Truss Wall House. Located in the centre of Doha City, it enjoys a fine view of the bay. Spaces are created to accommodate the owner's world-class collection of contemporary and ancient art.

The Soft and Hairy House in Tokyo (1994) made use of a planted roof, well in advance of their widespread introduction today. It was a modest house with a variety of undulating planted surfaces and sensual beginnings. These feminine forms extended themselves into the more ambitious design for the Doha Art Foundation in Qatar (2003), for the then Minister of Culture. Sat whale-like on the desert sands, alluding to myth and culture, this sensitive creature had a vitality that was born of function yet spoke of the seas of sand it rested upon. When engineer Cecil Balmond saw the proposal in Kathryn's studio, he commended its use of the ancient Arabic vernacular of courtyard for ventilation and thick walls for thermal mass. These functional and contextual projects, though built of concrete, reveal a pliable use of the Modernist material that, through docile and moderate form-making, reach out to the heart, not simply the mind or gut that seem to be the target of so much architecture today.

Kathryn's rural upbringing on a farm has instilled in her a deep appreciation of the countryside. It is something that she has been searching out in the city ever since. This is reflected in her drawings of London. Her cityscapes are not collections of buildings, but continuous flowing landscape-like spaces. The drawings show the frame of the city from which one can re-imagine the sky – so often obscured on urban walks by our looking downwards at asphalt, paving and enclosing buildings. Yet humans have the capacity to look upwards, and will do so given the opportunity to stop for a moment; pausing to appreciate the sky, wind, rain or sun. Kathryn's architecture frames these things and brings them back to our attention.

Ushida Findlay Architects with Michael Williams and Lesley McIntire, The Hill, Arts and Culture Proposal, London, 2006
Commissioned for the London 2012 Olympic and Paralympic Games, the client here proposed an art gallery presented as a theatrical experience. The art is to be enjoyed as a journey of installations and performances, arranged in four intertwining routes that combine to form a hill. The exterior surface is landscaped so that visitors can enjoy the view.

Ushida Findlay Architects, Truss Wall House, Tokyo, Japan, 1993
Cited as a canon of 20th-century architecture, the Truss Wall House was designed and built 20 years in advance of the current fashion of curved-form buildings. The project began as a technical commission from the owner of the Truss Wall system, a method of compound-curve concrete construction. It had been in use for many years in a figurative form, made to look like dragons, curtains and the like. Ushida Findlay Architects reinvented the system by creating an abstract free and flowing form, making the most out of the confined site.

Often the word 'genteel' denotes weakness in the minds of architects in the West. However, traditional Oriental culture and philosophy offer a less rigid and responsive approach that provides opportunities for engagement and continuity.

In Poolhouse 1 (2001), which was designed as a leisure wing for a listed house in the south of England, Kathryn made an effort to raise the roof of an indoor swimming pool. Its elevated interior belies a heavy thatched roof that is further elevated by being held on thin pilotis and enclosed in minimally framed glass panels. Here the experience of swimming is both enclosed from above yet immersive, in that one senses being below the bows of the roofscape. This immersion is further enhanced with warm lighting and a clerestory window, above which sit reeds and flower beds as a reference to the traditional use of living wildflowers and grasses that were once incorporated to bind the thatch in traditional Japanese houses and temples.

The compassionate nature of the pool house was continued in Poolhouse 2 (2009), an annex wedged between a Grade II-listed farmhouse and a barn in Buckinghamshire. More immediately contextual, it links separate parts of the family home. The experience of swimming here takes a new turn. The swimmer must swim around the pool to follow an easy curve – it is no lap pool. Like the previous pool house, this is a place of immersion and contemplation, where even the individual balusters in the balustrade, made of glass, glow below the weight of the handrail and ask that we stop to enjoy the moment. Here, the curve of the thatched roof is expressed as stepped. The zigzag character does not jar, due to the nature of thatches' woven curves and stolid wrapping. Its agreeable mild character gives an impression of lenient efficiency rarely associated with spaces of services, exercise and water. Our love of the clinical bathing experience in the West has often led to sterile, overly expressed services and white bathing spaces. However here, as in the bathroom of the Soft and Hairy House, a more forgiving and temperate atmosphere is evoked. This is reminiscent of Jun'ichiro Tanizaki's 'In Praise of Shadows' (1933),[3] a seminal essay on Japanese aesthetics, where the author extols the warmer, sensual and darker bathing experience of the Eastern bath-house over the standard clinical white-washed, reflective and glossily tiled Western bathing experience.

Ushida Findlay Architects, Poolhouse 1, southern England, 2001
The design of this indoor swimming pool and leisure wing of a Grade II-listed luxury residence was carefully crafted, employing local materials, and most notably a thatched roof, so that it would sit comfortably within the surrounding countryside. The planted roof was inspired by academic research into worldwide thatching techniques, adapting an ancient Japanese planted method. Poolhouse 1 received the RIBA Award for Architecture in 2001 and was mid-listed for the Stirling Prize.

Traditional Japanese thatch
From Findlay's research into different thatching techniques.

Often the word 'genteel' denotes weakness in the minds of architects in the West. However, traditional Oriental culture and philosophy offer a less rigid and responsive approach that provides opportunities for engagement and continuity. This adaptable mindset is apparent in the competition-winning design for the Grafton New Hall country house in Cheshire (2000), where the house's footprint resembles a giant dinosaur foot, and responds directly to views across a rural landscape. Despite its contemporary design, the house was granted planning permission in a sensitive countryside setting due to its originality. Its form, like that of the Kasahara Culture and Amenity Hall in Gifu Prefecture, Japan (2006), is simply a response to a love of the sun and the views available. This is not an artificially 'designed' architecture, but rather a scheme that can be regarded as a manifestation of the site's sun path and aspect. The spaces were shaped by Findlay's response to many aspects of the house's context. Rather than representing an idealised architectural assumption, they demonstrate a heartfelt desire to connect with natural elements and locality.

Rather than representing an idealised architectural assumption, they demonstrate a heartfelt desire to connect with natural elements and locality.

Ushida Findlay Architects, Poolhouse 2, Buckinghamshire, 2009
For this poolhouse designed and built to link two properties, the planning restrictions required that the extension be built on the existing curved-plan footprint. The client requested a thatch roof supported above glazed walls. Ushida Findlay Architects crafted the traditional roof form employing digital design technology.

Kathryn enjoys the 'thingness' – or tactility – of architecture and believes that it should speak directly to the inhabitant and viewer. However, as Elia Zenghelis once pointed out, 'architecture is dumb',[4] and it is this very simplicity that lies at the heart of what Kathryn tries to achieve. The quiet being-ness of the building allows the elements in the surrounding space to 'speak' or to have a chance to be seen. This instinct for how architecture might manifest itself and be imbued with a particular ambience is also enhanced by her love of construction and handcrafted materials. In the Soft and Hairy House she was part of the team that made the concrete balls that formed the floor of the bathroom. Here, the building process became a ritual. In some way this is similar to the traditional Japanese ritual of rebuilding timber structures; when temples have become tired they are destroyed and rebuilt on the same site by a new set of local builders. The act of rebuilding provides a revitalised and localised appreciation of the temple as architecture and as a sacred destination.

The lexicon of Japanese characteristics that Kathryn has adopted and adapted over time gives a poetry to her work that most Westerners regard as creative and original design. However, her design, like her love of cooking, relies on a beguilingly simple use of good ingredients found on or around the site that do not require fussy dressings or designs, or to be overworked. The minimal qualities of the pool houses stem from a modesty she first encountered in the pared-back work of Arata Isozaki when working in his studio on her arrival in Japan in the early 1980s.

Ushida Findlay Architects, Grafton New Hall, Cheshire, 2000
This competition-winning design broke the mould when it received planning consent for a contemporary country house on a greenfield site, and later became a model for changes to government planning policy.

Ushida Findlay Architects, Kasahara Culture and Amenity Hall, Gifu Prefecture, Japan, 2006

The form of this local culture and amenity centre in the tile-manufacturing centre of Japan employed local tiles and was formed to maximise passive energy strategies. The space is multipurpose, enabling activities ranging from art exhibitions to children's sports. The amorphous envelope extends to form a 'protective' arm that shades the building from the sun, with the glazing located to provide passive ventilation.

Another love of Kathryn Findlay's is language. Language, particularly Japanese, relies heavily, like her architecture, on context. The Japanese dictionary, the Kanji, includes multiple meanings for the same word. The correct or appropriate word relies on the speaker interpreting the context correctly, and from this context arises all that is needed. In some ways, therefore, the architecture, like the word, is to Kathryn less important than the context. She lets the ingredients and context do the talking. And this perhaps is one reason why she was reticent to write in this issue about her own work for this piece. She would rather that her architecture (the context of this text) speaks for itself. ⚙

Notes
1. Peter Cook in conversation with Kathryn Findlay, 2007.
2. Rory Olcayto in conversation with Kathryn Findlay, *Architects' Journal*, 19 February 2009.
3. Jun'ichirō Tanizaki, *In Praise of Shadows*, trans Thomas J Harper and Edward G Seidensticker, Leete's Island Books (Sedgwick, ME), 1977.
4. Elia Zenghelis, Lecture with Eleni Gigantes, University of East London, 1991.

The Japanese dictionary, the Kanji, includes multiple meanings for the same word. The correct or appropriate word relies on the speaker interpreting the context correctly, and from this context arises all that is needed.

The Couple.

The Pergola.

THE
LAND OF
SCATTERED
SEEDS

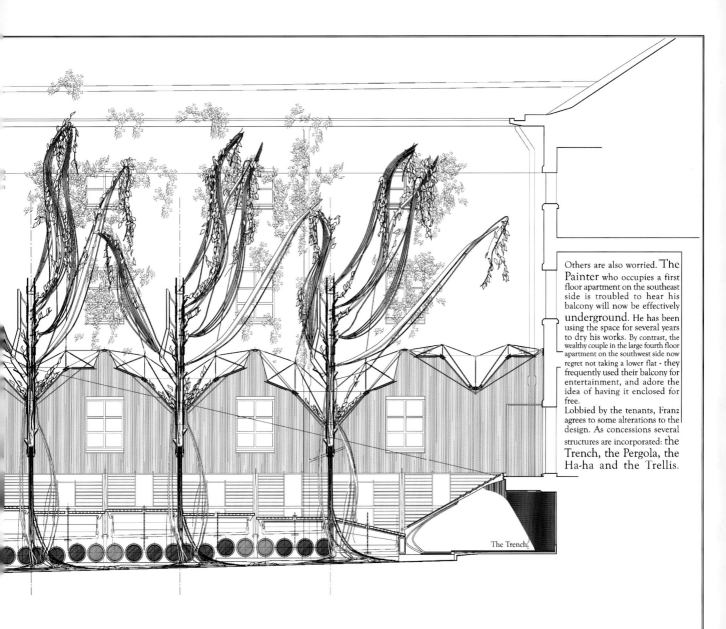

Others are also worried. The Painter who occupies a first floor apartment on the southeast side is troubled to hear his balcony will now be effectively underground. He has been using the space for several years to dry his works. By contrast, the wealthy couple in the large fourth floor apartment on the southwest side now regret not taking a lower flat - they frequently used their balcony for entertainment, and adore the idea of having it enclosed for free.

Lobbied by the tenants, Franz agrees to some alterations to the design. As concessions several structures are incorporated: the Trench, the Pergola, the Ha-ha and the Trellis.

The Trench.

Architect **John Puttick** is now responsible for leading Make Architects' work in China. His diploma project for the Bartlett School of Architecture, *Land of Scattered Seeds* (2001), featured here and on the cover, has now taken on seminal status. Produced in book form, a copy was purchased by the Museum of Modern Art (MoMA) in New York.

John Puttick, *Land of Scattered Seeds*, 2001
The vineyard is arranged as a series of horizontal strata, with glass canopies forming an artificial 'ground' level.

The Land of Scattered Seeds (2001) is an architectural story presented in the form of a book. The modern-day tale creates a self-contained reality that develops the idea of integration of modern city life with planting and agriculture. The complex relationships of life – social, ecological or economic – are studied and developed in miniature through the lives of a colourful cast of characters and their surrounding environment. These relationships are then played out through space and structure, revealing surprising connections between the most disparate things and creating a dense cross-section of urban and rural activities. No hierarchy of scale exists in the work, the smallest detail providing as many possibilities as the city as a whole. The book was developed for the final Diploma project at the Bartlett School of Architecture, University College London (UCL) and has subsequently been exhibited internationally. A copy was purchased by the Museum of Modern Art (MoMA) in New York for its collection.

The book investigates relationships between humanity and nature – the efforts of human beings to control the natural world, and the cold indifference of nature in return – and also the relationships between individuals as they attempt to find their place in the modern city. An orchestrated series of events sees a quiet provincial neighbourhood grow into a parallel economy based upon an increasingly daring vegetal invasion.

Beginning with the desperation of two brothers (Franz and Jorg), the inhabitants of a street in the centre of Graz, Austria, incrementally convert their environment into a patchwork of farms, vineyards and gardens. The ambitions of each character lead to conflicts and collaborations that evolve through the development of exquisite new constructions and the growth of plants. Nature – with ambitions of its own – constantly threatens to overwhelm them. The teeming life that results is microscopically documented in the book and further manifests itself in an intricate model concealed within the drinks cabinet of one of the leading characters.

At the outset of the story, utilising the only space they have available – the exterior of their apartment buildings – Franz establishes a vineyard, while Jorg grows pumpkins to refine into *Kurbisöl*, a kind of pumpkin oil used locally as a seasoning. Franz's vineyard is built in a narrow open courtyard. Organised into ecological strata, an artificial ground level is established at mid-height where water and leaves are collected for irrigation and composting. Above this level, vines are trained on delicate timber structures. Using the tendency of the vines to turn towards the sun, the structures gradually rotate during the day. Below the artificial ground, this movement is used to drive the process of gradually pressing the grapes to turn them to wine.

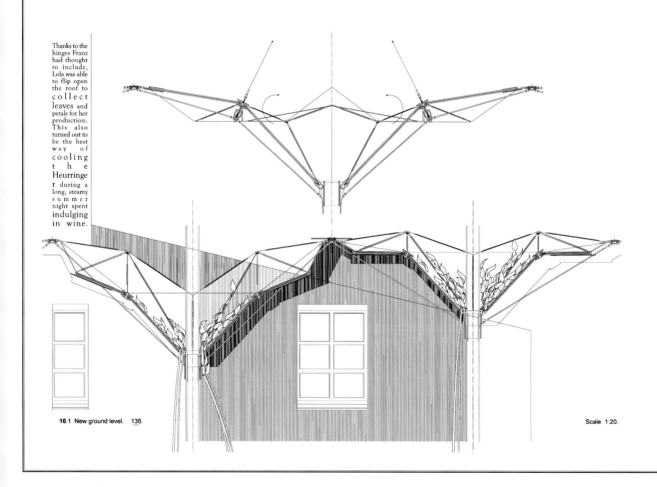

Thanks to the hinges Franz had thought to include, Lola was able to flip open the roof to collect leaves and petals for her production. This also turned out to be the best way of cooling the Heurringer during a long, steamy summer night spent indulging in wine.

16.1 New ground level. 136.

Scale 1:20.

The vineyard structures synthesise steel and glass details with the vines to form systems that move with the sunlight and seasons.

Within the gateway tunnel that forms the entrance to the courtyard, Jorg grows his pumpkins. The leaves are trained vertically on the building's facade to receive sunlight, while the pumpkins themselves grow in the artificial ground space of the tunnel. Here Jorg adds a wormery to his mini-industry to turn fallen leaves into fertiliser. During the summer, the structures supporting the leaves topple into the street forming an impromptu arcade beneath which the two urban farmers sell their wares. The brothers compete maniacally.

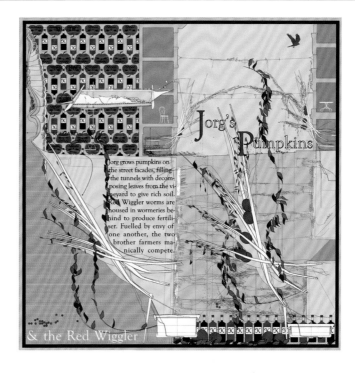

Jorg grows pumpkins on the street facades, filling the tunnels with decomposing leaves from the vineyard to give rich soil. Red Wiggler worms are housed in wormeries behind to produce fertiliser. Fuelled by envy of one another, the two brother farmers manically compete.

Jorg's Pumpkins

& the Red Wiggler

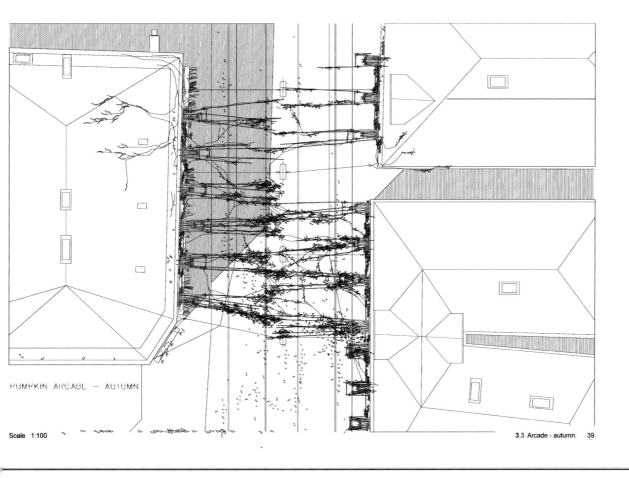

PUMPKIN ARCADE – AUTUMN

Scale 1:100

3.3 Arcade - autumn. 39.

Jorg establishes a pumpkin farm in the tunnel leading to his apartment building, in an attempt to compete with his brother Franz.

The leaves of the pumpkins are trained on the facade into the sunlight; in summer they topple over and form an arcade across the street.

43

Across the street live Olga and Florian who have retired from the Austrian civil service. Horrified by the vegetal chaos erupting in the area, the couple cultivate formal gardens on the facade of their building as an act of floral defence. An exercise in order and control, the pair develop a system based on pulleys that supports an array of essential gardening devices – for edging, aerating and moving the vertical lawn. Averse to any hint of industrial or technical aesthetic, Olga installs roses and gnomes to hide her equipment.

Lola, owner of the local hairdressing salon, proves more enterprising, taking the petals shed from Franz's vines to produce an enriching shampoo. To further soothe her customers, the entrepreneur also dries the leaves from the plants to create a herbal tea. The leaves are dried on the rooftop, sheltered by delicate lacy umbrellas that expand and contract depending on the quantities required at any particular time. To provide the honey required for sweetening the tea, Lola begins to keep bees in a self-heating hive in the attic of her building. Happily, the bees roam the farms below, providing rapid fertilisation.

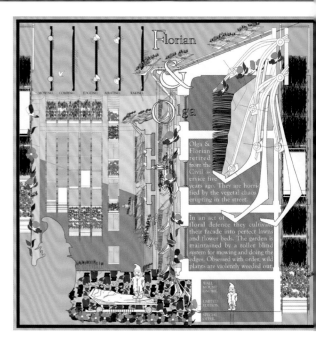

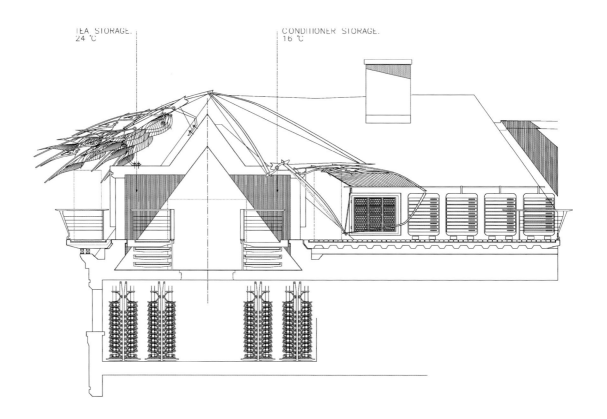

TEA STORAGE.
24 °C

CONDITIONER STORAGE.
16 °C

5.3 Tea / Shampoo Storage. <u>58</u>.

Scale 1:50

Cross-section through the apparatus of Lola, used to make honey shampoo and herbal tea for her hairdressing salon.

Horrified by the farming, Florian and Olga create a formal garden on the facade of their home in an act of floral defence.

As time passes the area flourishes, but soon the novice farmers find they have maximised the yield potential of the space at their disposal. A man of initiative, Franz proposes a solution – an ambitious irrigation scheme to feed water to the farms and increase the harvest. Lightweight tensile aqueducts are rapidly erected, carrying rainwater from the hillside onto the rooftops, the existing guttering providing distribution. The falls of some of the pitched roofs are used to create reservoirs, and algae are introduced to add nitrogen to the water for the benefit of the plants. Soon the roofs erupt into a riot of green and red.

With production greatly increased, Franz rapidly runs out of storage space within the courtyards along the street. To allow for expansion he colonises the spaces below the newly created aducts. Here he places his newly filled casks of wine, which are then encased in large timber shuttering. Over the years, wild plants grow up and combine with the timber, binding the construction together ever more tightly as the wine matures and gains in value. When the winemaker considers the vintage to have reached its peak, his team arrives and hacks open the casing.

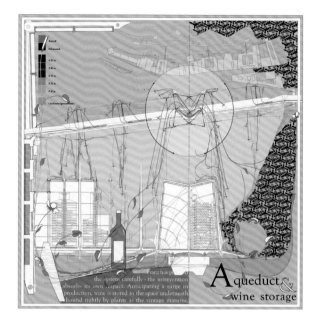

A queduct & wine storage

Over the years, wild plants grow up and combine with the timber, binding the construction together ever more tightly as the wine matures and gains in value.

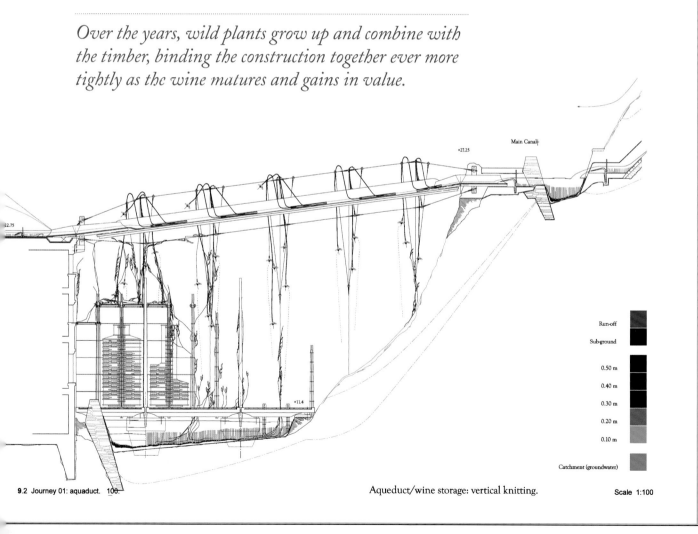

Run-off
Sub-ground

0.50 m
0.40 m
0.30 m
0.20 m
0.10 m

Catchment (groundwater)

9.2 Journey 01: aquaduct. 100.

Aqueduct/wine storage: vertical knitting.

Scale 1:100

h ambitions to increase his yield, Franz builds an irrigation tem to deliver a reliable water supply to the farms.

The tensile steel aqueduct spans between hillside and rooftop, delivering run-off water to the existing gutter system.

The resulting pergola screens their view of the vineyard, and creates a 'face' on which the upwardly mobile can project their image to the outside world.

Meanwhile, trouble is gathering for Franz at the vineyard. A numb[er] of the other local characters (Stefan, Helga, Hermann, Hugo and Wolf) are finding that the agricultural apparatus intrudes on their dail[y] urban existence. To placate them, the winemaker agrees to constru[ct] a number of structures to respond to their eccentric needs. Stefan and Helga – a fashionable young couple occupying an apartment at one end of the courtyard – demand a construction to beautify their balcony. The resulting pergola screens their view of the vineyard, an[d] creates a 'face' on which the upwardly mobile can project their imag[e] to the outside world. Their elegant cat Fifi is also delighted to disco[ver] many new ledges on which to fall asleep in the sun.

Stefan & Helga.

Stefan & Helga were delighted by the Pergola they had insisted that Franz construct. The space enclosed will be perfect for our Cocktail and Conasta parties, they agreed. Fifi loved her new space too.

Franz is forced to build structures as concessions to his neighbours – young couple Stefan and Helga demand a pergola to enclose their balcony.

Far from desiring increased social contact, Hermann is a quiet soul who lives together with his mother. His only friends are the birds he keeps, and the bustle of the growing farms has frightened this group of timid creatures. Always one to spot a win-win situation, Franz puts forward a compromise – he will build for Hermann a magnificent jewel-like aviary, in return for which Hermann will allow his prize hawk to patrol the courtyard (and conveniently scare off the wild birds who have been reducing the supply of grapes). For a period, harmony is achieved among the participants, and Franz and Jorg see beyond their differences and agree to work together.

Adversity is never far away, however. As autumn comes, heavy weather leads to floods and the dark threat of the phylloxera aphid – a microscopic insect that feeds on the roots and leaves of the grapevines – hovers over the vineyard. The intricate farming systems – so productive in better times – begin to work against the farmers. These twists-in-the-tale disrupt the short-lived urban-pastoral utopia and demonstrate the fragility of human plans in the face of nature. As the story comes to its climax, Franz, captivated by his new-found wealth, becomes tired of sharing his success and begins to develop new plans for the good life in a land of opportunity – the London suburbs. All the while, wild plants and birds continue to invade, and the struggles of Franz, Jorg, Florian and Lola continue. ⌀

Hermann the bird man.

For some time wild birds have stolen the grapes that Franz has cultivated. Gathering his courage, the timid bird lover suggests one solution – an aviary.

The aviary, built for Hermann, creates a delicate showcase for his magnificent hunting birds.

Architect **Marta Pozo Gil**, who leads the Sustainability Department at MVRDV, draws on a correlation between people's retreat indoors, with urban populations becoming increasingly divorced from nature, and the growing ambitions for 'green' cities and the ensuing benefits they bring to our quality of life. How might it, though, be possible to realise such a vision? Pozo Gil describes some of MVRDV's lesser-known projects that weave nature into the city.

WILD

MVRDV - WEAVING NA

CITY

URE AND THE URBAN

Now that the urban is an omnipresent concern, what is nature's role in debates, discussions and visions of the city?

Homo urbanus has in recent times delegated his quality of life to technology and consumerism, degrading the once more prominent role of nature for leisure and relaxation. We now spend much of our free time indoors – clear evidence of the retreat into the private realm we pursue. This migration indoors is a new trend, alienating us from nature and from other human beings, yet it fulfils our desires of control, comfort and independency. Paradoxically, the moment the middle classes emerge from their busy urban lives and have time to spend, they are too far away from nature to make proper use of it. Their only options are the superficial charm of city parks, or travelling to remote places in order to discover nature's real splendour. But could our urban fabric host culture, history, technology *and* the wild?

This divorce of humans from nature is also evident in the art world. After the Middle Ages, nature was an insatiable source of inspiration and research. Artists, writers and thinkers from the Enlightenment, Romanticism and Impressionism showed through their paintings and writings a harmonious interaction of humans with nature. The 14th-century Italian poet Francesco Petrarch claimed to be the first person since antiquity to have climbed a mountain to enjoy the view. And in the 18th century, painters like Joseph Mallord William Turner and Caspar David Friedrich emphasised the aesthetic qualities of the landscape. However, this 'living together' was to break down during the 20th century, as highlighted on the art scene at the time by the shift towards non-representational and abstract works.

It is an interesting and perhaps logical contradiction that humans turn to nature at the same moment they become urbanites. Nature-based experiences are therefore becoming a thriving tourist industry. National Parks and protected landscapes are immensely popular holiday destinations, however the sought-after authenticity and tranquility is being destroyed by these masses in their attempt to escape their daily urban lives.

Our current formula of developing urban areas while ignoring nature has proved unsuccessful, resulting in global warming, pollution, deforestation, unhealthy food production and aggressive tourism. Though cities are growing in terms of geographical area, number of buildings and population, the city as a public space is crumbling, with the urban fabric placing emphasis on the private realm where citizens can develop a sophisticated and comfortable life.

However, with increasing levels of air pollution, noise, traffic congestion and unsafe public places, 'green' cities are becoming more successful in global city planning competitions, and sustainable measurement frameworks such as LEED, BREEAM and GreenCalc are further developing a more holistic approach to the urban coexistence of humans and nature. But how can such ambitions be implemented? Can nature reactivate the city as a desirable public space? And can this be realised beyond the traditional park or sports field?

The presence of nature in a city contributes to its inhabitants' quality of life in many ways. It provides environmental services such as the purification of air and water, and limits noise pollution. It also encourages social interaction among neighbours, and can increase both physical and mental health, enriching urban life with emotions and meaning and acting as a stress reliever. Last but not least, it offers economic benefits, since natural elements attract people and investment.[1]

City makers therefore need to focus on a new organisation between the urban context, society and nature. The city can become a melting pot of multiculturalism and multi-naturalism for the benefit of all, creating adaptation among its human and animal citizens, as has already been documented in cities like London and New York. Urban areas need to preserve and encourage wildlife such as foxes, squirrels and seagulls that are adapting to the urban environment, and optimise the relationship between human beings, animals and plants. If we learn how to share our environment with them, we can enjoy watching these animal populations living in our midst, stimulating our natural instincts.

MVRDV's proposal for a new shopping centre in Barcelona an example of how nature can stimulate new experiences that can become part of our daily urban activities. For example, children running after squirrels and rabbits, experiencing the fresh air of the forest while parents do their grocery shopping. The forest on the roof also has a positive impact on its immediate surrounding a welcoming iconic element that brings new identity to the neighbourhood by integrating large and high-quality public spaces and purifying the air.

Despite all the positive aspects of nature, and its theoretical value and stunning beauty described in documentaries, many urbanites will never have the opportunity to experience it in an authentic way. How can we expect young generations to preserve nature in the future if they have not had the chance to enjoy it? Only if we develop a positive cohabitation of people, plants and animals will we become aware of its value and be encouraged to work for its protection and extension.

Imagine a natural neighbourhood where instead of nude and soulless plazas people can enjoy intensive vegetation. Imagine doing sports among nature, or stepping away from the hectic rhythm of urban life by walking through landscaped streets. Imagine schools with large vegetable gardens. Citizens could enjoy fresh air, relax, and be inspired. Children would develop their senses of challenge and adventure instead of playing in bland, artificial playgrounds.

The relationship between city planning, architecture and biodiversity needs a serious approach. Action to limit loss of biodiversity can be taken on many fronts: responsibly sourced materials can be used to minimise the impact on existing biodiversity patterns, and ecological design principles can be implemented at both building and regional scale to preserve local species. In the last decades, the global effort has continued to address the ideal healthy green city. However, many meaningful ideas remain only on paper – so many words, so little action. It is time for the *mise en scène* of thought to involve all the players: designers, engineers, politicians and citizens.

For the last 20 years, Dutch architecture and urbanism practice MVRDV has been contributing to this effort, often with theoretical arguments, but also with a range of highly pragmatic proposals. These include the Netherlands Pavilion at Expo 2000 in Hanover, a sequence of stacked Dutch landscapes, a mix of nature and building. However, the firm has also developed a number of other, much less well known proposals for a more symbiotic approach to architecture and urbanism.

Only if we develop a positive cohabitation of
people, plants and animals will we become
aware of its value and be encouraged to work
for its protection and extension.

MVRDV, Floriade 2022 World Horticultural Expo, Almere, The Netherlands, 2012
The aim of Almere Floriade 2022 is to create a green urban district that shows in great detail how plants enrich aspects of daily life.

Floriade will be a city that is literally green as well as ecological. A city that might even be autarkic: a symbiotic world of people, plants and animals. — Winy Maas

The Autarkic City

Can ecology and urbanisation come together to create self-sufficient societies?

The Floriade World Horticultural Expo takes place once a decade in the Netherlands. MVRDV's plan for the 2022 Floriade in Almere is not a temporary expo site, but a lasting green *cité idéale* – a green extension of the existing city centre. A grid of gardens on a 45-hectare (111-acre), square-shaped peninsula, each block will be devoted to different plants to create a plant library. The blocks are also devoted to different programmes, from pavilions to homes, offices, and even a university that will be organised as a stacked botanical garden, a vertical ecosystem in which each classroom will have a different climate to grow certain plants.

Visitors will be able to stay in a jasmine hotel, swim in a lily pond and dine in a rosery. The city will offer homes in orchards, offices with planted interiors and bamboo parks. In short, the Almere Floriade is a combination of programme and plants that will create programmatic surprises, innovation and ecology. The Manhattan grid – the symbol of modernity – transformed into a symbol of the symbiotic life of humans and nature. As Winy Maas, director and founder of MVRDV, states:

Floriade will be a city that is literally green as well as ecological. A city that might even be autarkic: a symbiotic world of people, plants and animals. Can this symbiosis between city and countryside offer essential argumentation to the global concerns regarding urbanization and consumption?[2]

Design Equality for All Species

Thinking of the city as the habitat of all species, and not only of people, can establish a more symbiotic relationship between buildings, land and nature, creating intriguing and exciting combinations of landscape and building functions.

In BiodiverCity, The Why Factory – a think-tank on urban futures led by Winy Maas – presents a vision of a city where architectural and urban design stimulates meaningful relationships between humans and other species. As The Why Factory explains:

[The study] will take off from … Deleuze and Guattari's thought that the opposition between humans and nature does not exist: human species within the biosphere is one among many. We will envision new engagement with natural cycles spreading beyond existing agriculture. We will design a new city embracing a democracy of people, animals micro-organism and minerals.[3]

Giovanni Bellotti and Erik Revellé, **The Wild City, Studio BiodiverCity, The Why Factory, 2010**
What type of city would animals love? How can we coexist with animals? BiodiverCity explores how both architectural and urban design could facilitate meaningful relationships between humans and other species.

Do Nothing

Regarding nature, often the best we can do is to do nothing. We need to regain a sense of humility when facing the overwhelming power of wild landscape. Is it possible to create a hidden urbanism that gives priority to nature?

During the design process of the Galije holiday resort in Montenegro, the decision was taken to combine exclusivity with a responsible sustainable embedding of the project in its surrounding landscape. The attraction of Montenegro's coastline could only be maintained by preserving its rugged beauty. As a result, the whole project was designed as an offset to the terrain, and covered with a blanket of the original landscape. Sadly, the 'invisible' resort was never realised – the envisioned guests apparently prefer the 'bling bling' of steel and glass – and Montenegro's scenic coast will soon look like the built-up shores of Spain or Turkey.

Continuation of Nature in the City

Urban nature is constantly competing against developments whose revenues are easier to quantify, therefore interest in bringing true natural spaces to the city remains poor. With creative and innovative solutions, this situation can shift to create a more collaborative approach. Strategies need to be developed that focus on merging manmade urbanisation with nature to maintain the charm of the city. But how and where can we create space for plants and animals to settle and develop among humans?

The Green Sofa is a respectful and exemplary response to letting nature take over the facades and plaza of a new development in Strasbourg, France. It increases the ecological value of the site and transforms it into a warm and genuine common space, introducing the striking beauty of nature and resembling a painted backdrop to the harsh stone surroundings.

The design of a dense urban masterplan for a new neighbourhood in Bordeaux will offer 3,200 homes, offices and urban amenities while also preserving the local biodiversity. In-between and inside the blocks are spaces for small parks, pocket gardens which function as platforms for local animals to coexist with people. Like cut-out buildings, these pockets literally investigate and realise three-dimensional gardening.

To quote Adolf Loos's maxim: 'Man loves everything that satisfies his comfort. He hates everything that wants to draw him out of his acquired and secured position and that disturbs him.'[4] Following this thought, humans love their houses and may hate the unpredictability of nature. On the other hand, though, homo urbanus seeks the excitement of the unknown and needs a certain degree of anarchy to stimulate him. How to combine the need of control with the desire of rebellion? Can the combination of city and wilderness bring together the rational and the unpredictable for the stimulation of people?

The old idea of splitting rural and urban ecologies is not attractive in either environmental or social terms. The

MVRDV, The Green Sofa, Strasbourg, France, 2012
Buildings and public space are wrapped with intense vegetation, creating a delightful escape from the frantic urban lifestyle.

challenge of providing lodging for people, animals and plants can lead to innovative and enriching spaces and experiences. However, this requires shifting the points of reference where current urban and architectural patterns would be neither applicable nor desirable. Overturning concepts are not easily acceptable, but smartly brought into practice can renew urban reality and go beyond its current repletion.

In order to design cities that satisfy all species, we need to create outstanding examples that give directions for a green future. Fortunately, the time will come where, instead of constantly reading statements such as 'buildings account for 38 per cent of carbon emissions and over 60 per cent of energy consumption', writers will delight in the efficiency of cities to purify the air, minimise water run-off, cohabitate with animals and, last but not least, foster the enjoyment of urbanites. △

MVRDV, Masterplan Bastide Niel, Bordeaux, France, 2010–
A new neighbourhood in Bordeaux offers a network of pocket parks/gardens that captivate nature at small scale. Each is made of different plants (geranium, wisteria, ivy) and different materials (wood, mirror, metallic net, brick). Each also has a different use (sports, reading, playground, biodiversity, community meetings and art installations), and theme: the Mirror Garden, the Bird Cage, the Sports Garden, Winery Garden, Wisteria Garden, Buxus Sculpture Garden, Geranium Garden, Tropical Garden and Vegetable Garden.

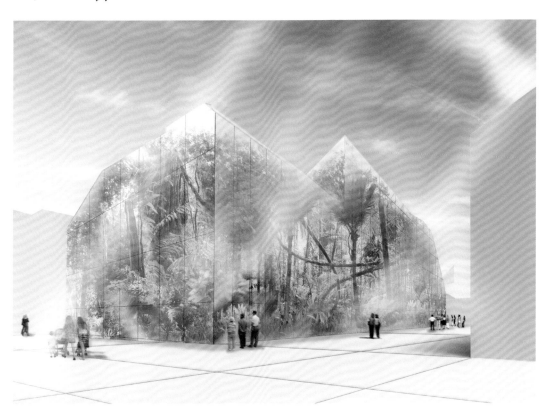

Man loves everything that satisfies his comfort. He hates everything that wants to draw him out of his acquired and secured position and that disturbs him. — Adolf Loos

Notes
1 Anna Chiesura, 'The Role of Urban Parks for the Sustainable City', *Landscape and Urban Planning* 68, 2004, pp 129–38: http://carmelacanzonieri.com/library/6123/Chiesura-RoleUrbanParksSustainableCity.pdf.
2 Winy Maas at the announcement ceremony of the winner of the competition for the Floriade 2022 World Horticultural Expo in September 2012.
3 The Why Factory, BiodiverCity, 2010: See www.thewhyfactory.com/?page=project&project=53&type=active.
4 In his essay 'Architecture' of 1910.

May Leung

SURVIVING VERSUS LIVING NATURE AND NURTURE

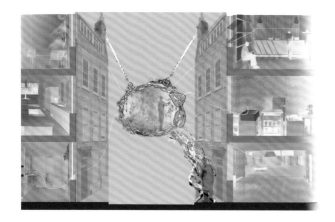

Today so many aspects of our everyday lives are dependent on nature, yet remain removed from it. Here, two speculative projects by the architect **May Leung** explore how nature can nurture in ways that space cannot, by creating self-sustainable systems to change the way that we think about production, consumption, leisure and the routine of our working lives.

**ay Leung, The Silk Cocoon Kiosk,
pitalfields, London, 2007**
ne Cocoon Kiosk is a self-sustainable eco-
od that integrates fish, mulberry plants
nd silkworms to produce silk that is sold
 the market on the pavements below;
ugged into neighbouring buildings for
ectricity and water, connecting to what
as once home to the silk weavers.

*Can the socially vitalising role
f nature be brought back to
ur urban lives to re-nurture a
ense of our human instinct and
ring us closer to the otherwise
gnored 'other' – neighbour,
nimal, plant or stranger?*

Hurricane Sandy's visit to New York connected people. Within this disaster's default setting, one's best place was with other people. This and the universal backdrop of Mother Nature are our true basic environments. Yet we have become disconnected from them.

Butterflies fly among flowers for nectar, spiders spin webs to trap prey, and humans once harvested land and hunted for food. As animals of nature and creatures of social comfort, our life in cities deprives us of the evolutionary instinct and beneficial trait that working together on the land can offer. Away from the very nature that supplies us with food, and the relaxing ambrosia of natural distractions, we seem only to tend to survival in the city; picture a bee in a concrete jungle without plants – it would soon die. Perhaps we should now be harvesting food for social purposes. It should not take a hurricane to bring us together.

Can the socially vitalising role of nature be brought back to our urban lives to re-nurture a sense of our human instinct and bring us closer to the otherwise ignored 'other' – neighbour, animal, plant or stranger? Perhaps we can find a little healthy indulgence that reconnects us back to each other and to nature that, as instinct suggests, offers a social, physical and mental abundance.

The Silk Cocoon Kiosk

Centuries ago, French weavers in Fournier Street in London's Spitalfields started an affluent silk trade. The 'kiosk' aims to revive this lost tradition. Initially, fish water provides nutrients to mulberry plants. Silkworms are insulated to feed on the mulberry leaves within the cavity walls. As the silkworm spins a cocoon, a single strand of silk is removed and threaded through a silk loom for weaving, leaving the leftover by-product of the silkworm to feed the fish, and completing the cycle. This integration of components forms a self-sustainable ecosystem, informing the design.

The structure begins to take the shape of a cocoon and has a biomorphic nature as it slowly adapts and behaves like the host silkworm. The silk cocoon is thus a hanging silk monument in the streets of Spitalfields. These mythical pods of nature are curious floating elements that coexist among us in the urban jungle, changing colour according to the seasons, glowing and churning from the looms at night. They live and breathe to create a beautiful, complex, natural layered abundance within our hard cityscape.

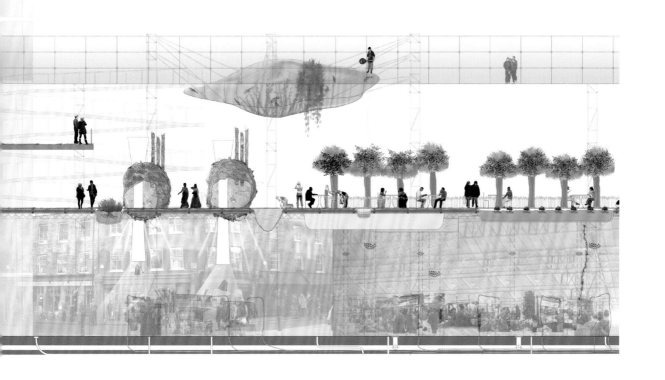

Penny X

Next stop Walthamstow

MICRO EXHIBITIONS ARE THE FUTURE

ALL CAN BE FIXED WITH LOVE.

May Leung, The Freeconomy – Learning Fields, East London, 2009
The project utilises wind turbines for power, gardening for produce and materials, a trading floor for bartering, workshops for crafting, and studios for exchanging skills. Each Freeconomist is identifiable via a website map that portrays his or her own personal trade.

Through learning and leisure, people are becoming skilled urban farmers; skilled in husbandry and intimate crafts using local produce.

FREECONOMY

It's about sharing your tools so you all can have access to all the tools under the sun without it costing the earth.
It's about sharing the skills you have learnt through your life and learning those you haven't.
It's about communicating face-to-face and phasing out technological communication.
It's about keeping money out of the equation.
It's about putting the soul back into society.

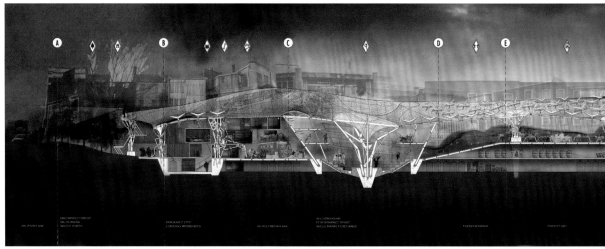

The Freeconomy – Learning Fields

In the heart of East London, the Freeconomists inhabit an old unused railway to build a shelter, harvest crop circles for food and cotton for warmth. The site opens up to the southwesterly prevailing winds, and they see the opportunity to create a roof for wind turbines to generate energy, and to build wall-mounted dovecotes and terraces of vines with climbers.

Through learning and leisure, people are becoming skilled urban farmers; skilled in husbandry and intimate crafts using local produce. A display of social life – a fecund space, a trading floor where harvests are exchanged, a carpenter bartering for linen from a cotton manufacturer – everyday life pours out onto the streets.

It seems that living a utopian dream can work; an alternative life that treasures rural streetscapes, creating a communal platform for living, playing and working. This freeconomy project encourages face-to-face communication and looks to small-scale local economies. But it also plugs into the grid, connecting people and communities on a global scale. ⌂

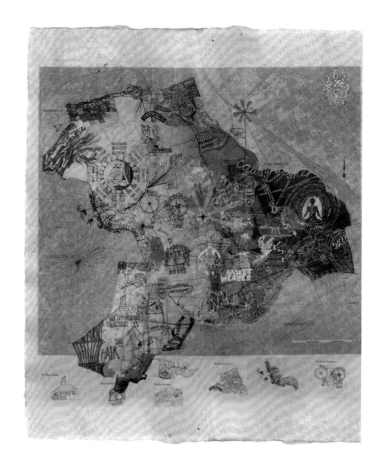

The apple tree doesn't ask whether you are deserving or undeserving, or whether you are going to nurture the soil in which it has laid its roots. It just gives.
— *Mark Boyle (2008)[1]*

LEARNING FIELDS
BY HACKNEY FREECONOMISTS
YEAR 2009 - 2020

Note
1. Mark Boyle, the Moneyless Man, is a writer and activist best known for founding the online Freeconomy Community, and for living without money since November 2008. See his blog at: www.justfortheloveofit.org.

Michael Sorkin

ORIGIN OF SPECIES

The renowned architect, academic and thinker **Michael Sorkin** reflects on the geneses of architecture, where it comes from and its current status, concluding that 'the idea of an architecture that participates in a collective stewardship and equitable sharing of the earth – and wears it on its sleeve – works for me'. He illustrates his article with some of his studio's work from the last two decades that has been inspired by nature in its iconography, embracing an entire menagerie of forms.

Nature creates similarities. One need only think of mimicry. The highest capacity for producing similarities, however, is man's. His gift of seeing resemblances is nothing other than a rudiment of the powerful compulsion in former times to become and behave like something else. Perhaps there is none of his higher functions in which his mimetic faculty does not play a decisive role.
— Walter Benjamin, 'On the Mimetic Faculty', 1933[1]

Organisms are the natural stuff of metaphor and ritual.
— Edward O Wilson, 'Biophilia', 1984[2]

Where does architecture come from? As social practice, it comes from politics, from persuasions of organisation and distribution. As human practice, it comes from ideas about comfort, safety and pleasure. As environmental practice, it comes from the configuration of economy and ecology, from reciprocal inseminations of global and local. As cultural practice, it comes from habit and history, from an accumulation of compacts and sanctions, from acts of collectivity. As artistic practice, it comes from convention and tradition, from the means at hand, from fantasy, accident, the unconscious and pure whimsy.

Art is the wild card in architecture and urbanism. It guarantees nothing: only its absence is a warranty. Of failure. But the present-ness of the artistic nowadays too often does not rise above branding, above distraction, above rapid devolution to the decorator version, the old but accelerating cycle of invention and co-optation. When the aggressive, destabilising shards turn out to be just another shopping mall, you know that game is up. But the balance is tricky: when the default was grey flannel, crazy design was a right riposte, and art's duty is to defend against all difference being sucked in by the consumption machine and its bottomless thirst for choice-less choices. Rejecting an art reified beyond interpretation, we keep looking for slack, for a slippery transcendence that invites us to enjoy, not just affirm. And to share.

Which brings us back to taste. While 'good taste' tends to be foul, the idea of systems does not. Shared taste cultures produce not just tactics of connoisseurship but – if participation is authentic – yield the shifting rituals of consensus (and objection) that keep appreciation lively and fluid. An avant-garde is indispensable for assailing complacency and privilege by constantly churning things up, by resituating the saturations of expression, and by providing protection for working out individuality by taking the piss out of priests. By definition, there is a struggle for this speaking space: resistance defines the new. But there is a difference between the freedom – even the incitement – to inventively share, and architecture's sorry categorical reflex to manufacture (and to haberdasher) grandees and groupies. The risk is elevating such demography to an absolute standard, the prison of so-called 'identity politics'.

Architecture always negotiates a terrain between its defining utility and expression, the frisson of some excess, including the excessive linkage of the two. But what more should a building say? We all speak in a language grounded in the grammars of modernity, the fantasy that meaning is 'objectively' produced, believe that architecture's effects can be measured and the dance and dancer distinguished. Yet we are bored by a trivialised idea of functionality that, claiming some higher rationality, grounds itself in the merely technical, and even the most 'objective' architecture seems invariably in thrall of something else's visuality, failing abjectly without the festive measure of the body. We do always (and aptly) ask: What does it look like?

Representation is the spectre haunting Modernism, and its worst involutions have emerged from idealist conceits for bridging the gap with abstraction, from trying to depict the conceptual, to imitate an idea rather than a thing. Modernism's enormous nose for technical aromas is largely the result of its increasingly marginal position in the actual scientific vanguard, producing flurries of wishful mimetic embodiment, flitting among metaphors – the geometrical, the mechanical, the

Animal Houses: Frog
1989

Three creatures – dog, frog and aardvark – from 1989 are part of a bestiary of projects through which I worked out a pretty literal, if completely unsystematic, interest in biomorphism. I cannot account for this predilection nor – given that these projects were self-generated – do I think it particularly interesting to speculate on its origins. There is obviously a point beyond which these questions are simply personal and shared or not. The only polemic is asserting a little otherness. The three houses do engage certain architectural specifics: symmetry, directionality and elevation. Vertebrates are invariably bilateral and so are these buildings, each a wee riff on a small range of variation within a fixed and essentially symmetrical envelope. I have always been interested in the way in which fixed forms accrete eccentricities, the way faces are never quite symmetrical, the meaning of the coming and going of zits and the swollen cheeks of toothaches. Modernist child, I have also always had an on-and-off Jones for aircraft and ships. The aircraft carrier *Intrepid*, anchored in Manhattan, has long been fascinating for the way in which its deterministic, rigorously symmetrical, hydrodynamic shape has acquired a bristling entourage of turrets, antennae, cranes and other apparatus that tilt any reading towards irregularity.

linguistic, the statistical, the genetic and other image systems produced within some sanctioned field – where form, however complex, could be considered immanent, not applied, and its authority grafted to the yielding body of building ('intelligent' building means never having to open the window).

This crisis of appropriation surely began when the technologies that, for millennia, had shared a legible physical and conceptual space with architecture – a common environment shaped by wind and weather and weight – began to accelerate away in a mesmerisingly rapid, dramatically visible, evolution. Aeronautics soared from the Wright Brothers (just decades from Will and Orville to Werner) to the moon in less than a century – while the Mother of the Arts debated the correctness of the strip window and piloti.

Architecture's anxious relationship to technology and its forms derives from engineering's exponential formal evolution within architecture's terrestrial meadows, from the impenetrable metaphysical grandeur of so much scientific speculation – who among us truly understands the Higgs – and from the increasing muteness and invisibility of contemporary technics, as our appliances lose their old Newtonian legibility clutter, and it all just looks Apple. Architecture searches for a way back in, but finds itself increasingly without, and cannot understand whether it is nature's intensification or its author. No surprise that architectural discourse has taken a biological turn in recent years, the over-determined result of its own culpability in the degradation of the planetary environment, and of the explosive growth of knowledge in the 'life' sciences, becoming an artefact of the contested intercourse of carbon and silicon, and the concomitant substitution of the simulated for the mimetic. The language grows more commutative: even as we nail the DNA code, biology ceases to be destiny as we dream of downloading the cumbersome wetware of consciousness onto a more durable chip.

One outcome of this anxiety is the feverish devolution of affinity onto simulacra of natural process. Parametric design (the automated variety: all design is governed by parameters), which models itself on 'natural' ideas about growth and evolution, is (depending on the designated constraints) both functionalism's heir (still talking about 'programmes' and 'functions') and its antithesis (shit, forgot to control for empathy, for the undisciplined instincts of the hand, for the wandering shepherd who instigates the pastoral – can the sheep be electric?). If it is useful, though, it will not be just as a way of mechanising imagination, creating a special plenitude of monkeys to sit at infinite Underwoods, a private gene pool spinning out an endlessness of variations until some satisfying freak – carefully vetted for the current standard of unthreatening non-conformity – pops up for us to choose. It will be as the means to craft amazingly precise and variegated responses to architecture's greatest challenge, the necessity for the radical sustainability that will guarantee planetary survival should we fail to overcome the blind fetish for growth understood as mere multiplication. Earth (meaning us) is in the balance.

Every work of architecture participates in a mimetic economy, and the object of building's representational desires seismographs the sensibility of both architect and culture. Whatever the originating 'reality', theories of mimesis – from Plato to Benjamin to Auerbach to Taussig to Robin Williams –

What we need more than ever now is both a theory and a practice of excess, the rampant particularities — small and large — to fight the great multinational culture machine.

Pickle (Hanseatic Skyscrapers)
Hamburg
Germany
1989

We were doing some work in Hamburg and decided to quickly imagine a couple of skyscrapers there. Not much to be said about them, save that the 'Pickle' was designed well before the London Gherkin, and that it is lifted up to acknowledge the double-ended essence of a cucumber. The other project, the Fiddlehead, suggests an idea about a close-packed multiplicity of slender towers in a single 'building'.

Beached Houses:
Slug, Carp and Ray
Whitehouse
Jamaica
1991

The Beached Houses – slug, carp, and ray – were designed for a site near the sea in Jamaica and are another exercise in biomorphic bilateralism. Although they are inspired by marine creatures, rather than mammalians, they beg the same questions of symmetry and, in the case of the carp, of elevation above the ground. They differ from the Animal Houses in having much lighter frames and were to have been built from small members with a light – and lightly stressed – metal skin.

The Beached Houses engage the idea of representational motility via a somewhat more fluid – if mild – asymmetry, and via the idea of the wiggle, an integral distortion of symmetry produced via respiration, motion or some other life process. Thus, the tail of the ray is caught as it swings to swim, the carp begins to turn, the slug creeps along. The project called for three houses of each type and the site plan catches them in a net of palm trees.

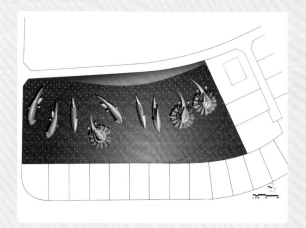

Turtle Portable Theater
1995

The motif of body and shell is carried on by the Turtle Theater, which evokes a creature that succinctly expresses this dualism. Here, though, the body in question is multiple: the bodies of the people who shelter within for performances. And the shell is itself no turtle's rigid box, but a thin fabric membrane kept up by air pressure. The commission came from a troupe of travelling puppeteers, and the theatre is designed to be demounted and shipped from place to place.

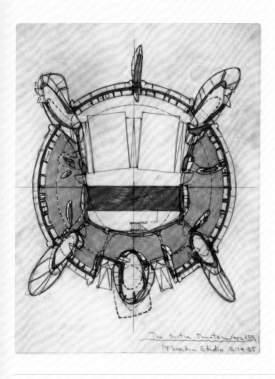

Somewhat more complicated than a simple inflatable combining hard elements with soft, this movement from one venue to another was not – in emulation of its eponymous muse – intended to be altogether swift.

deal with imitation, with the perceptual or artistic mediation and transfer of some authenticity from the environment in which it is produced to another in which it is represented. Modernism's fantasy was low rent, founded in the self-annihilating (if elegant) dream of an asymptotic relationship between the represented and the representation, an aesthetic of efficiency, which tried to represent the criteria of the disciplines from which it drafted its procedures. It imagined visual purgation as a way to evacuate and control stray meaning, the fantasy of no surplus, just the function ma'am.

What we need more than ever now is both a theory and a practice of excess, the rampant particularities – small and large – to fight the great multinational culture machine as it seizes and markets every difference, creating a field of total abstraction in which no origin, no connection, no authenticity is left undiminished and remains truly vital. Against this, life must fight back both in terms of the glorious and inventive urgencies of building truly sustainable architectural cultures that will help save the planet, and in the creation of artistic forms that do not simply shock but satisfy – an architecture of empathy. And this is the great and simple point of the art historian Wilhelm Worringer's flash of insight, the brilliant binarism of empathy and abstraction, which recovered representation by infusing it with an explicit sense of the social, understanding it as a profound site of the shared. Do I overstate if I feel, when I sketch a building that looks like a beast, that I am connected to the connections of my ancestor, deep in the cave, daubing a picture of a mammoth on the wall in the dark?

We have been working on this question for a while. The eruption of post-modernity and its restoration of repressed representation was, among other things, a rebellion against the hegemony of a club of withholding dads. Not simply had their imaginative well run dry, but the dominant minimalism on offer proved itself incredibly congenial to both high-corporate and low-social-welfare projects and was rapidly blanketing the earth with incredibly impoverished product. The Postmodern riposte (founded in the funkadelic visual style of the counterculture and the hypertrophic outpourings of consumerism) was salubrious for a time. The situation has now grown both worse and better. Worse, in that frisky form-for-form's-sake sanctions anything via some twisted libertarian gyre, a death to distinction. Markedly, the recuperation of Modernism itself as a set of historical practices allowed such disappointments as neo-Constructivism, which is to say the forms without the politics. On the up side, though, this opening up offers space for expressions more ardently developed or more grounded in arguments that challenge static ideas of mimesis with the dynamism of purpose and empathy.

Kind of a long-winded apology for some buildings that look like animals, vegetables and rocks. Sometimes, when I show this work at lectures, people want to hold me to account for it; they will not accept simple explanations, whether reassurances about the presence of performative qualities that serve – and extend – the necessary programmatic or environmental defaults, or more personal accounts of riveting sights or the simple evolutions of form or the un-severed bond I feel for my childhood dog, Mackey, her shapes, her colour, her movement, her puppy love. The risk: kitsch, a hand grenade (or a fart) directed at minimalism and exclusionary piety, reverts to kitsch.

Godzilla
Tokyo
Japan
1992

Godzilla was informed by both cultural and morphological fantasies. It is one of a number of works for unvisited sites, otherwise a no-no but an important way of pump priming and purification, and this was a warm-up for my first trip to Japan. At one level, this skyscraper is meant as an intensification of Tokyo-ness, an upward surge of the convulsively energetic disorder of the city. Inspiration comes too from Godzilla, the figure of monstrosity, the distillate of Japanese post-nuclear anxiety, from the idea of mind transmuted into animate matter. More conventionally, the building is meant, like the teeming districts of Tokyo, to be a dense model of mixed use. Lower limbs house larger functions, department stores and theatres. The middle portion (this tripartite organisation is nothing if not traditional) is for offices and the commerce of the open floor plate. Upper levels are for fabulous housing, floating above the city, and this skyward bulge is inflected to capture views. At the base, the creature simply lands in the imagined disorder and interrupts the confusion, establishing a new car-free quarter from which tendrils of green extend to colonise other areas for energetic quietude.

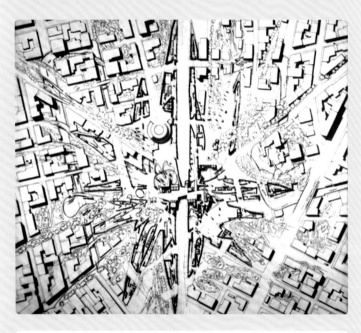

More enduring is a longer history of architecture's romance with 'nature'. I love those set-back skyscrapers from the 1920s and 1930s (Ralph Walker rocks!) that aspired to be mesas and mountains and whose sun-mottled forms remain indelible, great. When building *is* a mountain, there is nothing especially twisted about the logic of having it look like one: architecture is an extension of the earth by other means. I collect those fabulou 'scholar's rocks' from China, totally charmed by their obvious incipience as architecture. Why should not an object be as affecting as an algorithm?

Organisms too are irresistible points of departure. Creatures are champions of symmetry, autonomy and family – beautiful, alive, recognisable, evolving, breedable. Of course, a building can be all of that without looking like a fish or a paramecium, but why not? The question eternally remains the wiggle room between form and use, and it is important to be wary of the compulsion to abstract away, deracinating the form, maybe retaining some of the language as a memento of our ability to think freely, analogically. On that side, now lies the whole popular and hugely picturesque terrain of 'biophilia' and 'biomimicry'. The latter, in particular, re-instigates the Modernis dream of a functionalist mimetics, the idea that there are processes in nature that can be literally copied to yield productiv results in other fields and, simultaneously, to pull our habits of knowing into a more integrated alignment with this new version of universal consciousness.

While such a vision is fraught with dangers, particularly for the political, which it risks discarding in favour of f***ing our dear mother Gaia, the idea of an architecture that participates in a collective stewardship and equitable sharing of the earth – and wears it on its sleeve – works for me. Once the nature of this connection is established, many useful traditions open up, embracing the Arcadian strain in modernity's romantic antecedents, the lush histories of agriculture, the native sustainabilities of traditional building, the whole project of terraforming – the self-conscious cultivation of the loops of planetary survival that literally sustain us. In the end, everything we do is biomimicry, after all.

But let us not be so hard on Gaia: higher consciousness can always do with a little religion and its rituals. These are always mimetic and can be judged for the abstraction – one might even say poverty – of their content. The forms of propitiation, instruction, flattery and obedience that define them evolve, are contested, wither and morph, and the vitality of worship can be read in both the stillness – the emptiness – and the elaboration of its expression. This is not to overstate the importance of the work for which this small introduction is a warm-up, but simply to assert that the taste culture that undergirds it has, like any other, been produced not from blind preferences, but from both considered and unconscious ones, and that the forms of that consideration mingle psychology, purpose, propaganda, pleasure and tomfoolery. These are projects that choose to depict things both beloved and endangered, arguments for a kind of diversity and latitude. And there is an attempted rejoinder to the idea tha the theorisation of architecture's content is necessarily arcane, that its meanings must devolve on smaller and smaller sites, suggesting a spurious precision that well-ventilated, worshipful goofiness aims to resist. The real scales of architecture's role in distributive justice and ecosystem health – the city especially

Wagga Wagga Town Hall
Wagga Wagga
Australia
1995

There is a certain obvious efficiency in the serpentine form, like the convolutions of the intestines that both pack great length into a minimised area and – in the case of an architecture that is porous – allow lateral communication between runs of building that wrap into parallel. This project, in plan, combines both linear bilateralism with a series of organs – larger spaces – that occur periodically, with influence in both plan and section.

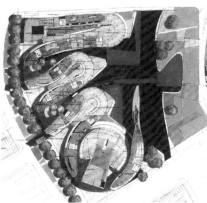

The Sheep Out West
1990

The Sheep continues the interest in animal figuration, bilateralism, elevation and directionality, but with greater interest in the skeleton. Here, the structure is a multiple dwelling: a series of distinct units sit within a skeletal structure. The prosody of the solution depends on the way in which the units – or organs – interact with the frame in a process of evasion, deferral, engagement and support. We aimed at a Chinese puzzle, a set of three-dimensionally conceived, interlocking units, providing both a reliable array of bedrooms and baths, but also a certain resistance to conventional inhabitation. This is meant too as a reflection of the situation of this building in New York's SoHo, the *locus classicus* of loft living and its idealisation of largely unpurposed space. The elevation of the building on legs is, in part, due to its siting on an existing parking lot, but the principle, as with the Animal Houses, is also derived from the spirit of pilotis and the same notional 'light lie on the land' that comes from barely touching it. This relationship to architecture's eternal dialectic of excavation and elevation – the cave versus the tree house – is an abiding problematic in any architect's work. As ever, this is a matter of preference and performance: the underground house generally sacrifices insolation for insulation. Like the Animal Houses, the Sheep also enjoys a migratory latitude and – although it was designed to 'fit' a specific site (a still undeveloped parking lot on Canal Street), we have placed it in a variety of settings with no attendant deformation of its practicality, although, perhaps, with certain shifts in its meaning.

House of the Future
1999

In 1999, in anticipation of the millennium, we were commissioned to do a couple of projects under the rubric 'the (blank) of the future'. The House of the Future was solicited by *Time Magazine*. We understood that the nuclear family was becoming increasingly atypical and so designed this as a modest co-housing project. A series of double units share living machines and there is also a detached, collective space for dining and working together. Formally, it does look like a version of the architectural future minted at least half a century earlier.

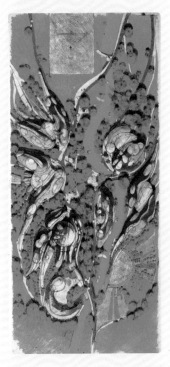

Herd Houses
Friedrichshof
Austria
1997

In 1997, we were hired to work on the re-purposing of a former commune in the Burgenland, not far from Vienna. Under the charismatic, if dictatorial, leadership of the artist Otto Mühl, the place had flourished, even burgeoned: its mainly Austrian and German members had been required to keep their day jobs and tithed the gain to the commune. The operation collapsed when Mühl was sent up the Danube for the exercise of his self-arrogated seigneurial right to deflower the girls of that commune at an age that eventually became perverted. In its day, however, a handsome piece of land had been acquired and a series of communal buildings constructed, although in an architectural style more apt to a barracks for the Hitler *Jugend* than a temple of the avant-garde. Left with this resource, a group of recovering members decided to open the place up to outsiders, imagining that the beautiful site would attract weekend residents.

Our first scheme was rejected as overly grand, even Disney-esque and so we went on to think about a group of houses of identical design for one corner of the property, facing fields beyond. While clearly creatures, their origins are not entirely clear. All have what are clearly bodies and tails, which secure their dual orientation to a perimeter road on the outside and the communal campus within. Each house features a cellar for the storage of the excellent wines produced in the region and to serve as a thermal buffer. The barrel roofs that vault over the main living areas are clearly carapaces, and these shells suggest an idea about hard and soft, about shelter and sheltered. They have lined themselves up in a kind of compact site-plan degree zero, and their viewing exposures are principally at the ends, facing fields across the way at their heads and park-like communal space at their tails. Side views are minimised, but clerestory windows bring in light and allow cross-ventilation.

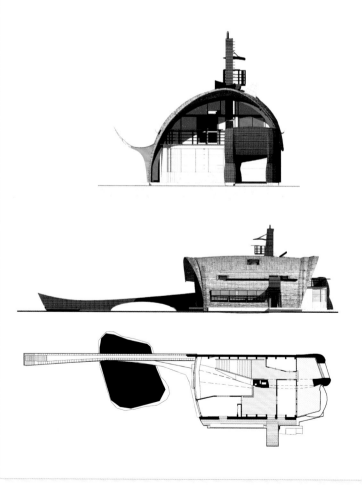

Snail Emergency Shelter
Fukushima
Japan
2011

In response to an invitation following the tsunami in Fukushima, we produced this quickly deployable emergency social space – also based on an inflatable membrane – in which a variety of shared activities might take place in a sheltering community. The project recognises that the standard repertoire of urgent shelters often fails to include much attention to communal, social spaces, thus the Snail was intended to serve smaller groups – children doing their homework, extended families sharing a meal, fans watching a football broadcast. Tensile elements serve as lighting standards and vamp antennae, giving, we hoped, an aura of friendliness to a dispirited gathering, especially the kids.

The Jellyfish
Tianjin
China
2009

A commission came our way for a small, 'signature' 'seven-star' hotel. We were not sure, exactly, what was implied by this inflationary emblem of status, but the programme called for rooms of insane generosity, luxury that seemed a stretch for a development at an unprepossessing edge of Tianjin. A tower was a logical solution given the small site and the commanding views of the huge artificial lake at the centre of the Disney-esque site plan. The hotel sits on a little beach and is adjoined by two small private clubs. The building takes the form of a jellyfish and aspires to its wiggly-ness and luminosity. To reinforce the message, there is a big jellyfish aquarium in the lobby.

The building's organisation is straightforward, with a lobby at ground level, business facilities and a spa up one level, a shaft of hotel suites above that, and the whole topped with a domed restaurant, private dining and karaoke rooms, and a bar. The tentacles are largely ornamental, but do provide some security against lateral forces.

Skyscrapers With Chinese Characteristics
Beijing
2012

The inhabited mountain is surely the hoariest metaphor for the skyscraper. From Gaudí to Taut to the great Deco towers of pre-depression New York to *Close Encounters of the Third Kind*, there has, for a multitude, been an irresistible impulse to model towers on mountains and mesas. I have long shared this tooth, driven to obsession by visits to Cappadocia, to the American West and, perhaps most strongly, to Ha Long Bay in Vietnam where the concatenation of cones and their doubling in reflection simply blew me away. Unseen, but often conjured, is the landscape of Guilin in China with its similarly ethereal peaks rising in the river mists.

Of course, the sacrality of mountains is a staple of faiths descending from the foggy past, and perhaps nowhere is the mountainous more exactingly revered and aestheticised than in China, where it has been reverenced for yonks in Taoist, Buddhist and Imperial traditions and figures in systems of geomancy, pilgrimage and, of course, representation. Scholar's rocks are domesticated, miniature mountains, geologic *bonsai*. My fascination with them has to do precisely with their incipience as architecture, their weirdly habitable-looking tectonic and their irresistible character as almost-skyscrapers.

– are happily the subject of much discussion elsewhere. Sometimes, though, forms just gotta have fun.

Mea culpa, I still associate progress with experiment, insubordination, innovation and the circus. The question is where these qualities are located in the larger territory of practice, where they sit on the continuum of the personal and the political: it is possible to speak about architectures that are more and less public, and it seems clear that the valence of their meaning shifts. While I have a passing interest in the psychoanalysis of the boudoir, I am inclined to leave it alone theoretically: the scales of privacy enjoy a more absolute freedom than the more collectively constrained scope of the neighbourhood or the city. Although no architectural object can live outside its social meanings and effects, there is a sliding scale of the nature and importance of those effects based on the extent of their influence: sometimes a building is just a building.

This is not to slight the consequences of aggregation, the multiplication of private exception in the public realm. In an era of elevated environmental consciousness, no building can escape the consequences of its use of energy and materials, or of the waste it produces – here minimalism still definitely cuts it – or of other down- and upstream effects that it embodies. As the income gap grows and the critique of the prerogatives and piggishness of the one per cent becomes more articulate, we cannot fail to acknowledge that architecture, especially when built, is an increment in the system of distributing privilege, and answerable. People who live in McMansions must get stoned.

So, here are some buildings the studio has designed over the years that resemble other objects that populate the planet. You may find them homely, stupid or brilliant, but these obvious influences are not offered as ipso facto authenticating. All I insist is that the meaning of a house that looks a bit like a frog is neither necessarily shallower nor deeper than one inspired by a *Proun* (or a prune) than the trace of an atom in a cloud chamber, a topological surface, a factory or ocean liner, or the microscopic structure of zirconium. It is all just somebody's taste. *De gustibus.* ᐁ

The following people were instrumental, over the years, in developing these projects and producing the drawings and models shown: Kent Hikida, Makoto Okazaki, Andrei Vovk, Jie Gue, Ying Liu and Luoyi Yin.

Notes
1. See Margaret Lock and Judith Farquhar (eds), *Beyond the Body Proper: Reading the Anthropology of Material Life*, Duke University Press (Durham, NC), 2007, p 130.
2. Edward O Wilson, *Biophilia*, Harvard University Press (Cambridge, MA), 1984, p 101.

QUIT THE GREY LIMBO AND RETURN TO PARADISE

In three projects, **Mathew Cannon and Mascia Gianvanni** of FutureScape Studio explore the possibilities of alleviating the mundaneness of urban life through the introduction of the absurdity of nature, which brings 'joy and laughter to the stressed worker'. Devices range from a sardine on the London Underground and a giraffe in the office to injecting a sublime, painterly light into the city.

A giraffe in the office, a lion in the waiting room, a hippopotamus in the toilet. The absurdity of an unthinkable nature misplaced in a mundane urban scenario creates chaos in a world made of rigid rules and preconceptions of what urban life is.

Time off, weekends and holidays recharge the stressed mind as they offer opportunities for variation. A chance for new challenges, relaxation and laughter. Perhaps the cure for stress should not be sought away from the urban environment, but should be incorporated in our daily lives as a way of absurd living that will integrate the natural world into areas of the otherwise grey and monotonous work environment.

There is now evidence that pet prescriptions actually work as a method of reducing stress levels. Research has demonstrated that when dog or cat owners were asked to perform a difficult arithmetic task, they showed less stress in the company of their pets than in the company of a friend. Other studies have found that owning a pet relieves depression, reduces blood pressure and triglycerides, and improves exercise habits, all of which can lower the risk of a heart attack. Studies even suggest that having a pet might aid survival after a heart attack. 'Among other things, animals contribute to raising self-esteem, significantly lowering anxiety levels, improving attitude toward others and opening lines of communication.'[1]

A great list of qualities for a 21st-century city.

The three projects explored here use the absurdity created by the introduction of nature in its opposing urban scenario. Fish Out of Water explores how a commuting sardine goes unnoticed in the chaos of the rush hour. Specifically prescribed maintenance and care of exotic flora and fauna within the working space is explored in Quit the Grey Limbo, and the cure for stress is approached in What is the Cure for Time Sickness?

Fish Out of Water

Giant stuffed animatronic anchovies roam the Underground. Crammed in like sardines, the fish out of water infiltrates the 6pm commuter routes carrying a briefcase and shuffling to the integrated iPod. For the few that notice him, smiles spread – a rare sight on the Jubilee line.

The sardine is a new space balancing juxtapositions between the everyday and the ludicrous. In a world of dualities and the dilemma between living in the city or countryside, the pastoral world can only be perceived in its condition of total opposition, which is the city.

Canary Wharf exists as a preprogrammed space designed as a habitat for a preprogrammed mind. The space is perceived as numb and has no spontaneity or discovery to be enjoyed by the human beings. The need for a challenge can be provided constructively by using an absurdity placed in an otherwise mundane scenario. This challenge is designed to stimulate and liberate the people who use this space daily, providing an exciting, humorous release from the everyday routine. The area is notoriously stressful, and research has shown that the main sources of work-related stress are heavily linked to demands for hitting targets and deadlines, long working hours, increased workloads and frequent changes in busy schedules.

a world of dualities and the dilemma between living in the city or countryside, the pastoral world can only be perceived in its condition of total opposition, which is the city.

Matthew Cannon and Mascia Gianvanni/FutureScape Studio, Fish Out of Water, Canary Wharf, London, 2007
this page and opposite: Roaming sardines. Observations on the 'un-thinking' termite lifestyle.

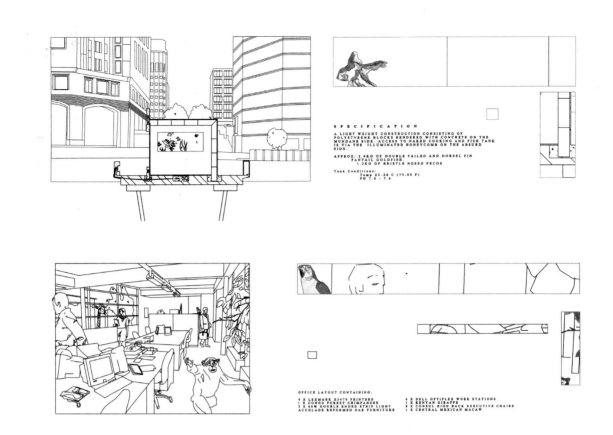

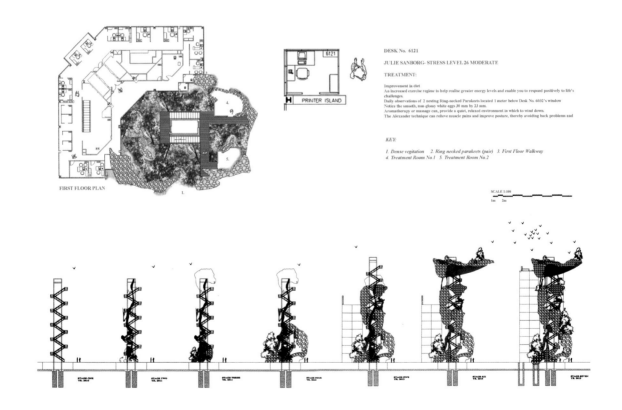

**Matthew Cannon and Mascia Gianvanni/FutureScape Studio,
Quit the Grey Limbo, Canary Wharf, London, 2007**
top: 1.2 kilogrammes (2.6 pounds) of bristlenosed plecos. A lightweight construction consisting of polystyrene blocks rendered with concrete on the mundane side. Access to the naked cooking and fish tank is via the illuminated honeycomb on the absurd side.

bottom: Proposed Vertical Sanctum: five years' evolution. Desk no 6121, Julie Sandborg, stress level 26 MODERATE. Treatment: daily observations of two nesting ring-necked parakeets.

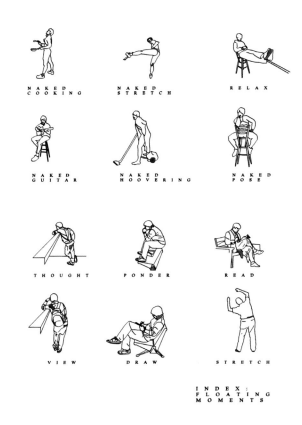

NAKED COOKING

NAKED STRETCH

RELAX

NAKED GUITAR

NAKED HOOVERING

NAKED POSE

THOUGHT

PONDER

READ

VIEW

DRAW

STRETCH

INDEX:
FLOATING
MOMENTS

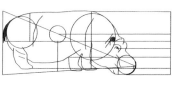

PROPORTIONS OF THE HIPPOPOTAMUS

PROPORTIONS OF THE HUMAN BODY

Quit the Grey Limbo

Would the cleaner mind having to wipe the giraffe lick off the windows? Or should the giraffe clean the windows when the cleaner is sick? Would the life of the office worker be enriched if every evening before shutting down his PC he had to remove a particularly stubborn parakeet from his office? Can parakeets survive weekends without vegetable samosas and Moroccan-style couscous salad?

Paradise returning to the grey limbo may be the cure for stress. Blurring the boundaries between the outer nature and the inner workplace could be seen as a solution; floor plans are now designed for both human and chimpanzee.

As the English novelist John Fowles remarks in his book *The Tree* (1979): 'the historical evolution of man into a predominantly urban and industrial creature, an un-thinking termite' explains how the workers execute monotonously their never-changing, repetitive tasks.[2] These 'un-thinking termites' could quit the grey limbo if only exposed to a moment of irrationality. This would require a substantial introduction of humour in the otherwise sluggish and boring environment.

The humour would come in the form of absurdity. Canary Wharf offers the perfect blank canvas where the absurdities will immediately stand out. The Vertical Sanctum project tries to set a challenge, but more importantly provoke laughter.

The two opposing realms are incorporated within the walls of the Vertical Sanctum, each side designed to tease and create absurd situations. On one side the space is designed for the mundane: areas for hot-desking, filing and other tedious tasks. The other side takes you from work to leisure, home, fun and relaxation, containing spaces for bizarre activities including naked hoovering and photocopier machines for office parties.

A transition between work and play.

top and centre: Floating moments. Naked cooking, naked stretch, relax, thought, ponder, read, naked guitar, naked hoovering, naked pose, view, draw, stretch. Proportions of the human body compared to the proportions of the hippopotamus.

bottom: Transition between work and play. The internal features of the hollow honeycomb housing include: 2 x reticulated giraffes (*Giraffa camelopardalis reticulata*), of which 1 x female, 9 years/Kenyan; 1 x male, 3 years/East Ugandan; and 1 x wet-room area equipped with 4 coloured shower heads. Office parties are also situated on this side, complete with Toshiba DCP8040 photocopier.

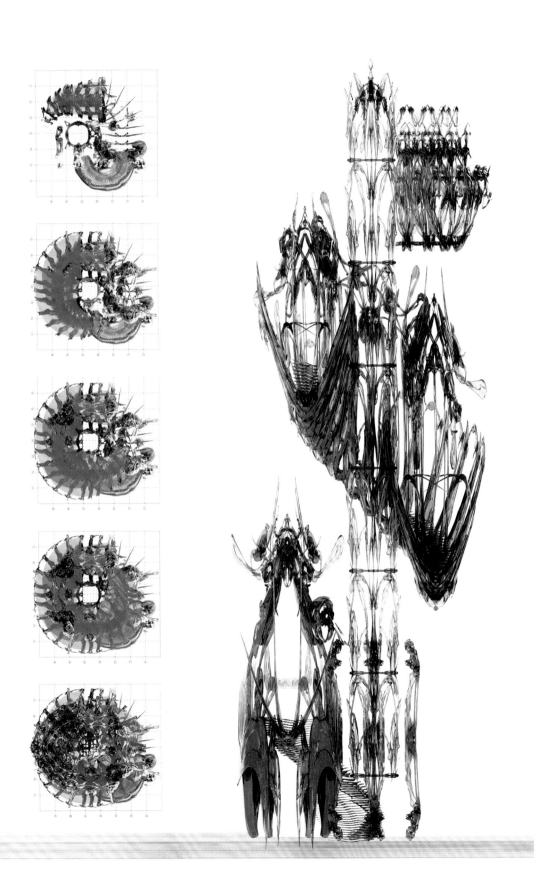

Matthew Cannon and Mascia Gianvanni/
FutureScape Studio, What is the Cure
for Time Sickness?, Porchester Road,
London, 2012
below: Atmospheric gallery. Details on the
light illuminating the path.

opposite left: East elevation. Broken
chandeliers become the basis for a
future computer.

opposite right: Analogue computation
of light. Fog reflecting the subtle light
particles illuminating all things.

What is the Cure for Time Sickness?

From then on I was irredeemably lost as a townsman. I have had to spend long years in cities since then, but never willingly, always in daily exile.[3]

A bathymetric bath crafts light and atmospherics, converting them into the cure for time sickness. A space set within a Joseph Mallord William Turner landscape, a quiet misty place, deep inside the city, yet a place where time is slow, a place for play, a place where light becomes magic.

Shakespeare's Prospero was the only one who could have filled the sky with sunshine or tempest at his will. To the painter, light is the magic agency with which he models all his forms, makes the very air visible and creates space itself.

Light. A phenomenon or effect, it is the medium of vision. Light and its radiant forces, heat and vibration, constitute the extreme opposite of all other states of matter. Solids, liquids and gases all either have a fixed boundary or are quantifiable as a volume of space. With light we reach the physically infinite. With light there are no fixed points or material particles, there is no state of matter, only an infinitely muted and agile motion.

Light unifies everything by illuminating all things. This description implies abilities more than 'light' alone is capable of. Light penetrates everywhere as a mode of vibration, effecting all other matter, reflecting from their surfaces. The landscape artist is dealing with these systems within his canvas. There are points of convergence and separation, reflection and absorption, and it is only through the vision of the audience that these modes of external vibratory forces are transferred into a burst of splendour and illumination. Light is seen as the most significant connection between the material and virtual worlds; illumination is used as much as a physical phenomenon as a spiritual idea. Light is the most ethereal, subtle and the most spiritual of all elements.

The landscape painter's active surface may be seen as an analogue computer rendering moments of light, a kind of 'unconventional computing'[4] device that perceives the impalpable light and processes it back into the painting as a material. The analogue computer gives materiality to the light, transforming it into matter. For the painter, the canvas is the analogue computer that accepts the input of light in the variation of time. The computer is built using the ever-changing, vibrating, constantly moving force that is light. The painting is a surface, computed as a space made of reflected light. The depth, as in a computer screen, is imagined. Turner's paintings have the illusion of depth and motion; by moving light through colour he invokes a spatial field. ◮

Notes
1. Karen Allen, PhD, a medical researcher at the University of Buffalo, conducted a 1999 study of 48 stockbrokers who had high blood pressure and concluded that owners of a cat or dog had lower blood-pressure readings in stressful situations than those who had no pets. 'When we told the group that didn't have pets about the findings, many went out and got them,' she says. Lois Baker, 'Pet Dog or Cat Controls Blood Pressure Better than ACE Inhibitor, UB Study of Stockbrokers Finds', 7 November 1999: see www.buffalo.edu/news/4489.
2. John Fowles, *The Tree*, Aurum Press Ltd (London), 1979, p 46.
3. Ibid, pp 18–19.
4. Unconventional computing – computing by a wide range of new unusual methods, including optical, chemical, quantum and wetware computing. These interdisciplinary research areas strive to go beyond the standard models.

Liam Young

BRA
NEW

UNDER TOMORROW'S SKY

VE NOW

IS A FICTIONAL, FUTURE CITY.

Under Tomorrow's Sky is a fictional future city. For the project, speculative architect **Liam Young** assembled a think-tank of scientists, technologists, futurists, illustrators and science-fiction authors to collectively develop this imaginary place, the landscapes that surround it and the stories it contains. The city forms a stage set for a collection of fictions, emerging infrastructures and design experiments. It is an imaginary landscape extrapolated from the wonders and possibilities of emerging biological and technological research. Here, speculative fiction provides a critical tool, which is visionary in its trajectory while provoking us to examine some of the most pertinent questions facing us today.

We wander through the city. It has been a long time since we have seen anyone else. Looking around I see a place I know but at the same time find utterly unfamiliar. She asks me where we are.

I reach down and pick up a small round badge from the rubble. I pin it to her coat. It reads 'I have seen the future'. It was a souvenir once given to visitors after their voyage through time on board the General Motors Futurama ride at the 1939 World's Fair. Sitting on an automated conveyor belt, visitors would travel through a model of the city of tomorrow, its skyscrapers, traffic lights and tangles of interchanges and expressways. Where once stood the imagined landscapes of what the 1960s might bring is now a dusty ruin, an archaeology of the social and technological ambitions of the time in which it was made. She tells me she has seen this place before, in vintage YouTube clips, tinged with the quaint nostalgia of retro futurism and archive footage.

We walk on, past the rusted hulks of an Archigram Walking City now propped up on blocks. Their massive metal bodies have been stripped down to their frames by futurist souvenir hunters and steel salvage yards. The dozers have moved in on what remains of the cruciform foundations of the Radiant City. The concrete corners have been worn smooth from decades of skateboard grinds and graffiti-removal teams. We can make out the words 'LC was here 1967' amidst the scrawls and tags of an age of archi-tourists. The players of New Babylon have closed their show, packed their ladders and drawn the curtains. The endless grid of the Superstudio Supersurface that once stretched beyond the horizon has been pulled up and resurfaced. The blinding white has mildewed and tree roots have skewed and cracked the measured lines. The tiled landscape has been reclaimed and now paves the food courts of distant strip malls, soaking up spilt milkshakes.

Liam Young, Under Tomorrow's Sky stage set model, 2012
Working with special-effects artists from such films as *Alien*, *Sunshine* and *Blade Runner*, Liam Young and the architects of Tomorrow's Thoughts Today have built a room-sized movie-miniature model of the fictional city.

I tell her we are walking through a city of [fa]iled utopias and constructed dreams. It is a [ci]ty of nowheres, a city of follies, a city of our [ho]pes and dreams, our most intimate desires [an]d our collective fears. As I tell her about [th]e city I once knew, I can tell she is listening [bu]t does not really believe everything I tell [h]er. She has stopped trying to recognise the [ci]ties I am describing. 'There is melancholy [an]d relief as we give up any thought of [kn]owing and understanding them.'[1] They [w]ere not built for that purpose. They were [no]t designed to be constructed, just to be [ex]plored, discussed, loved and hated, fought [ov]er or wished for. The cities of what is to [co]me do not just anticipate, but actively shape [te]chnological futures through their effects [in] the collective imagination. Only in these [ac]counts of the future are we able to discern [th]rough the walls and towers destined to [cr]umble, the dreams to remain unfulfilled, the ['tr]acery of patterns that we can follow through [th]e unmappable'.[2] Beyond the dig sites of [ob]sessive paleo-futurists, the speculative city [ha]s been abandoned for some time now. 'It is [a] desperate moment when we discover that [th]is empire, which had seemed to us the sum [of] all wonders, is an endless, formless ruin.'[3]

We walk on and come to the edge of a [ne]w territory. We look out across an evolving [fr]agment, in endless construction. There the [tr]aditional infrastructure of roads, buildings and public squares is giving way to ephemeral digital networks, biotechnologies and cloud computing connections. The physical city we know is destroying itself. She asks: 'Is our city still a city anymore?' At the very least the architect of this city is being redefined. Architects once speculated on the impacts of industrialisation and then mass production. Walking through this history of futures suggests to us alternative forms of spatial practice whereby architects can again play a critical role in speculating on the implications and consequences of emerging technologies. As the economy collapses and the city is reshaped, the future is beginning to become a project again. We have come to this part of the city at the beginning of its life. We begin a short walk through the landscapes of this brave new now. It is not clear to her what is fact and what is fiction; the two intertwine.

Daniel Dociu, *Urban Tectonics*, Under Tomorrow's Sky concept art, 2012
[abo]ve and previous spread: Game concept artist Daniel Dociu was invited to join the [Un]der Tomorrow's Sky think-tank and contributed digital paintings that developed [th]e design discussions.

Hovig Alahaidoyan, *Coastline*, Under Tomorrow's Sky concept art, 2012
above top: Hovig Alahaidoyan, a concept artist for film and games, worked with the Under Tomorrow's Sky think-tank to develop a collection of narrative vignettes set in the future city.

She whispers while we listen to the whistle of computer cooling, and the bleeps of mirrored beasts living their luminous lives. The fish were biting and below the ocean the blinking lights of the coastal supercomputer brain gives the water a curious glow. Where we once pumped mountains of sand into terraformed worlds lost under the weight of mirrored towers and air-conditioned oases is now the site of this new construction. 'The new city is standing out in the tidal currents of the Persian Gulf, flanked by dusty oil-drilling ghost towns and the wreckage of the Iranian Trucial States.'[4] She stumbles across the uneven ground; it is faceted and abstracted, a computed geology, part rock pool, part sedimentary construction site, glistening with moisture, bathed in light from street-lamp stars. The buildings seem to grow, and decay, and grow again from the fertile grounds of cities past. 'It is a system generating its own soil, creeping out into the sea and expanding its own volume through the metabolism of its ecologies.'[5]

'All this industry is biotech, quiet, subtle, done at room temperature, a vast urban swallowing. Rippling tubes feed spasming streams of mud through kidney-like membranes and filters. Electrical power comes from long, flexing, tidal tentacles, nervous strands like huge jellyfish tethers.'[6] Through it we glimpse the clouds beyond, thick with seeds of bacteria. There is a materiality to the weather here. She brushes the spores from her hair. Years before we had visited the blue cities of India. The subcontinent superpower has gone global and now influences the markings and urban patterns of this new city. Buildings tessellate down the landscape, an inhabited geology of crevice rooms and public valleys. They told us the colour-washed walls were believed to keep down the infrastructural insects that swarm across the city's pharmaceutical gardens.

'The boundaries of the body are disintegrating and we are becoming one with the city.'[7] Virtual interactions become a part of our physical selves and crowd-sourced computation becomes a new kind of magic. 'They lived within an urban computer. They never talked into mobiles or typed on keyboards. Instead, they gestured. They behaved like silent film actors, stagey and posed, playing to the cameras. To interact with their cityscape, they waved their arms, wiped, swiped, pointed, prodded, nodded and stared at things. This avatar of the city was a live architectural model, spatially identical to the genuine, physical city. The map of the city and the real territory of the city were entirely co-existent.'[8] Here the interbreeding of biology and technology has exploded infrastructure into bits, to roam the earth in an architecture of everywhere. 'It is a walled city of invisible barriers patrolled by drone networks, mapped by satellites, a protected endemic ecology fringed by a bacterial quarantine zone.'[9]

She had her binoculars slung around her neck. 'The first laboratory birds we see as we step upon the rugged shores of the big city is a flock of Gaseous Canaries, and their joyful notes are the first to salute our ear. High above the rooftop vents drift the Green Throated Sentinel Canaries, bioengineered to be sensitive to increased levels of CO_2. The luminescent plumage of the Roseshift Canaries catches the sun as they fan their tails and sing sharply in the clouds of nutrients. Large patches of luminescent algae dapple the surface of this wild country; and the moisture in the air is so peculiarly penetrating that it brings to mind a fearful anxiety for the future. The song brings with it a thousand pleasing associations referring to the beloved nature I was told about in my youth, and soon inspires us to persevere in our curious enterprise.'[10]

It has been some time since we had left the city of faded futures. Above us the night air rumbles with a low hum. A flickering flock of pirate Internet drones scans across the skyline. As a mobile network infrastructure, the flock broadcasts its signal in a luminescent cloud, fading in and out over the city.

High above the rooftop vents drift the Green Throated Sentinel Canaries, bioengineered to be sensitive to increased levels of CO_2.

SINGING SENTINELS

am Young, Geoff Manaugh and Tim
aly (illustrations by Paul Duffield),
nging Sentinels: A Birdwatcher's
ompanion, 2012
is fictional guidebook describes a
esigned infrastructure of bioengineered
rds that monitor the air quality of the
ear future.

In the bowels of the earth, coal miners once hammered rock to the twitter of canaries that lived beside them, their changing bird song a warning alarm for a dangerous gas leak. These animal sentinels watched over our energy industry and kept us safe. Over our post-carbon cities, the atmosphere is thick with the gaseous legacy of these years of fossil fuel use. Echoing across our near-future landscape, is designed a new infrastructure of signing sentinels as bioengineered birds once again monitor the air for us. Altered bird songs ring out as a soundtrack to the anthropocenic spaces of tomorrow, an elegy for a changing planet.[11]

ELECTRONIC COUNTERMEASURES

Liam Young with Superflux, Eleanor
Saitta and Oliviu Lugojan-Ghenciu,
Electronic Countermeasures,
GLOW Festival, Eindhoven, the
Netherlands, 2011
Drifting through the city is Liam Young's
flock of GPS-enabled quadcopter
drones. In response to the network
shutdown that occurred during the Arab
Spring, the drones broadcast their own
Wi-Fi web forming a nomadic pirate
file-sharing infrastructure.

Fabricated from repurposed components that were originally intended for aerial reconnaissance and police surveillance, a flock of GPS-enabled quadcopter drones broadcast their own Wi-Fi network as a flying pirate file-sharing infrastructure. They swarm into formation, broadcasting their pirate network, and then disperse, escaping detection, only to reform elsewhere. The flock becomes a highly site-specific means to create peer-to-peer communication. It is a nomadic architecture, 'a roaming infrastructure built from digital broadcast rather than steel, a drifting island of information'.[12]

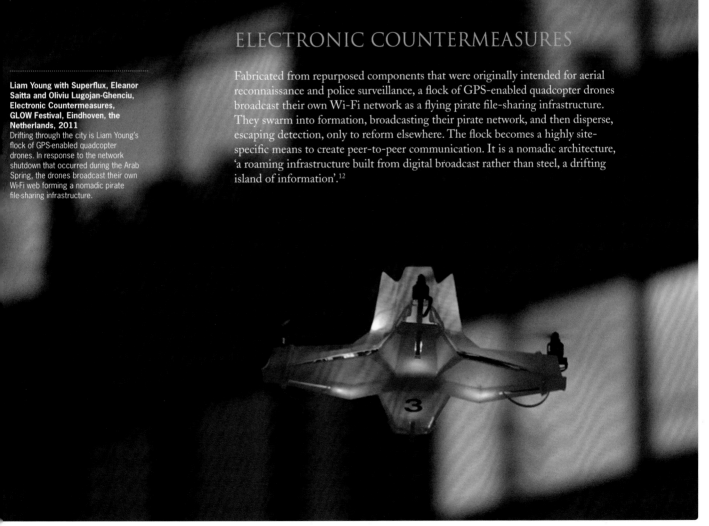

SPECIMENS OF UNNATURAL HISTORY

Catalogued as a collection of still lifes, stuffed and mounted taxidermy robots, curios, trophies and exotica, Specimens of Unnatural History is a near-future bestiary of designed and engineered biotechnical creatures, architectural beasts, robotic infrastructures and hacked military devices. Throughout history we have always invented monsters and myths as our way of coming to terms with phenomena we do not quite understand. The bestiary plays on the possibilities of the emerging field of synthetic biology and presents new hybrid creations as a way of coming to terms with our strange new world.[13]

Liam Young, Electric Aurora, Migrating Forest, Nomadic Silk Factory and Augmented Ferret, Specimens of Unnatural History, 2011
Catalogued as a collection of stuffed and mounted taxidermy trophies, Specimens of Unnatural History is a near-future bestiary of designed and engineered biotechnical infrastructures.

Following the intensity of the electromagnetic spectrum, a swarm of cybernetic fireflies map the network strength across the sky. As we look up in wonder, our faces bright in the rolling glow of a Wi-Fi aurora, caught in the light is a companion swarm of moths tethered to a nomadic silk factory herd that is spinning its glistening web across a field in the valley below. Shepherds track the herd's GPS tags. Here the processes of silk production are taken out of the textile factories and returned to the landscape. Scurrying about underfoot forests of young trees rustle past us following the weather. The migrating forest chases climate change across the globe in the dimming light of a day yet to come.

It is comforting to know these beautiful unnatural specimens have made it here with us. After nature their songs still sound and the air smells sweet. What we realise is that there is no nature anymore, and perhaps never really was, at least in the sense that we culturally define it. We tried to think of a new word for it. We still have not found one. What we see is technology, engineered systems, augmented environments and invisible fields. On our walk through this history of futures we see how the imaginary city once, and now again, plays a role in developing new cultural relationships with the inevitable by-products of industry, a changing climate and the anthropocenic world.

Some of the people we meet on our walk through the brave new now are swept up in what the city could be, others are reserved and look on with caution. It is a place of wonder and of fear. We make friends, we hear their stories, and we share their lives. I have not walked these streets before. What things may come Under Tomorrow's Sky? ᴆ

Notes
1. Extract rewritten and adapted from Italo Calvino's *Invisible Cities*, Vintage Press (London), 1997.
2. Ibid.
3. Ibid.
4. Extract from 'My Pretty Alluvian Bride', a short story by Bruce Sterling for Under Tomorrow's Sky.
5. Rachel Armstrong, transcript from the Under Tomorrow's Sky public think-tank at the MU Foundation, Eindhoven, 2012.
6. Extract from 'My Pretty Alluvian Bride', op cit.
7. Rachel Armstrong, transcript from the Under Tomorrow's Sky public think-tank, op cit.
8. Extract from 'My Pretty Alluvian Bride', op cit.
9. Bruce Sterling, transcript from the Under Tomorrow's Sky public think-tank at the MU Foundation, Eindhoven, 2012.
10. Extract rewritten and adapted from John James Audubon's entry on the American Robin in *The Birds of America*, 1841.
11. *Singing Sentinels: A Birdwatcher's Companion*, fictional guidebook by Liam Young with Geoff Manaugh and Tim Maly (illustrations by Paul Duffield), Mediamatic Gallery, Amsterdam, 2012.
12. Electronic Countermeasures was originally developed for the GLOW Festival, Eindhoven, the Netherlands, 2011. It was created by Liam Young with Superflux, Eleanor Saitta and Oliviu Lugojan-Ghenciu.
13. Specimens of Unnatural History is an ever-growing collection of future taxidermy originally developed by Liam Young for 'Landscape Futures', curated by Geoff Manaugh at the Nevada Museum of Art, Reno, 2011.

Some of the people we meet on our walk through the brave new now are swept up in what the city could be, others are reserved and look on with caution. It is a place of wonder and of fear. We make friends, we hear their stories, and we share their lives.

Under Tomorrow's Sky was developed by Liam Young with the MU Foundation, Eindhoven, 2012. The Under Tomorrow's Sky think-tank included Bruce Sterling, Warren Ellis, Rachel Armstrong, ARC Magazine and Paul Duffield. Under Tomorrow's Sky is an ongoing project that will be further developed as Future Perfect, curated by Liam Young for the 2013 Lisbon Architecture Triennale.

DIRTY FUTURES

Geoff Ward

Not only do bacterial cells in the human body outnumber human cells, but human habitation leaves microbial traces in the air and on surfaces. With these facts in mind, architect and academic **Geoff Ward** re-examines recent perceptions of 'the dirty' and recasts the natural in architecture in relation to it.

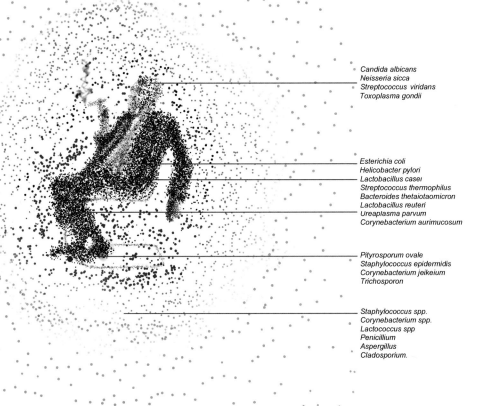

Candida albicans
Neisseria sicca
Streptococcus viridans
Toxoplasma gondii

Esterichia coli
Helicobacter pylori
Lactobacillus casei
Streptococcus thermophilus
Bacteroides thetaiotaomicron
Lactobacillus reuteri
Ureaplasma parvum
Corynebacterium aurimucosum

Pityrosporum ovale
Staphylococcus epidermidis
Corynebacterium jeikeium
Trichosporon

Staphylococcus spp.
Corynebacterium spp.
Lactococcus spp
Penicillium
Aspergillus
Cladosporium.

OR HOW I LEARNED TO STOP WORRYING AND LOVE MOTHER NATURE

Geoff Ward, Human Biome of Stars and Microbes, 2012
It has been long known that many of the elements that make up our bodily tissue originated within the nebula of dying stars many eons ago. Newly developed techniques of analysis have shown that the number of microbial genes in our bodies outnumbers our own genes by a factor in excess of 100 to one. The connections with our environment, near and far, are becoming steadily clearer.

In the film *Powers of Ten* made by Philip and Phylis Morrison and Charles and Ray Eames in the mid-1970s, we are taken on a whirlwind tour from the furthest reaches of space to the innermost components of the human genome. While this short movie still stands as a compelling account of the universe we inhabit, it neglects to mention the pivotal role of microbial flora and fauna as essential components of ourselves and of our environment.[1] As biological organisms, our existences are intimately and fundamentally entwined with a host of natural systems and processes. In addition to interaction with our wider environments, these complex relationships occur within our bodies and even within the cells of which our bodies are composed.

Far from being autonomous creatures, we are present as a complex and richly varied 'biome' in which bacterial cells outnumber our human cells by more than 10 to one, and bacterial DNA to human DNA by more than 100 to one. With these statistics in mind, it could be fair to say that we are only 10 per cent human.[2] While much of this microbial complement is made up of various species of bacteria assisting in the digestion of food and maintaining the health of the gut, the human relationship with microbes can be far more intimate. For instance, the presence in the brain of the protozoan *Toxoplasma Gondii* (in 10 to 12 per cent of the UK population) is responsible for subtle alterations to behaviour in those infected.[3] Further to this, energy transfer within all of our cells relies upon organelles called mitochondria. These are thought to be derived from free-living bacteria that lost their independent identities far back in evolutionary history. We are not only made of stars, but of microbes too.

This view of the human body as a mutualistic assemblage of disparate species stands in marked contrast to the traditional concept of us as autonomous physiological islands that simply require an alert and efficient immune system for the speedy recognition and destruction of all alien species. Furthermore, our 'microbiome' extends to our local environment, and leaves traces in the air and on surfaces telling of our inhabitation, thereby blurring the boundaries of what is 'us' and what is 'other'. This shift in awareness brings to mind Mary Douglas's famous observation that 'dirt is matter out of place',[4] and prompts a reassessment of the desirable state of matter and the conditions to which one's notion of 'dirt' takes on a culturally subjective valency. This view also challenges the notion that our environments can ever really be as minimal and clean as the Modernist dream would have it. We must look, then, at how the reframing of the 'dirty' has been approached in the recent past and how this can be used to develop a new and more pertinent relationship with the 'natural' in architectural and cultural discourse.

The 'dirty' as an object of artistic scrutiny, while at odds with the 'hygienic' Modernism that took root in the architecture of the early 20th century, was by no means unknown in other branches of the arts at this time. Marcel Duchamp was sufficiently interested in the accumulation of dust on his *Large Glass* (1915–23) that he lacquered it into place to retain it permanently as part of the work.[5] In literature, French poetry of the late 19th century makes frequent reference to the decayed and the unclean, notably in the work of Charles Baudelaire. Fifty years on, this had a marked influence on TS Eliot's *The Waste Land* (1922), and decay was also a subject Eliot returned to in *Four Quartets* (1943).

We must look, then, at how the reframing of the 'dirty' has been approached in the recent past and how this can be used to develop a new and more pertinent relationship with the 'natural' in architectural and cultural discourse.

It was not until 1958, however, that any coherent rebuff to the rational in architecture was forthcoming; in the form of Friedensreich Hundertwasser's 'Mouldiness Manifesto against Rationalism in Architecture'.[6] Here, the architect railed against 'the tyranny of the straight line',[7] and sought to rescue nature (that is to say, real nature, not a manicured and 'cooked' simulacrum) from its banishment by modern architecture:

When rust sets in on a razor blade, when a wall starts to get mouldy, when moss grows in a corner of a room, rounding its geometric angles, we should be glad because, together with the microbes and fungi, life is moving into the house and through this process we can more consciously become witnesses of architectural changes from which we have much to learn.[8]

Hundertwasser's practical proposal was that 'a decomposing solution should be poured over all those glass walls and smooth concrete surfaces so that the moulding process can set in'.[9] Later on, he returns to the topic of the human relationship with dirt and, more specifically, with excrement, with his piece 'Shit Culture – the Sacred Shit' (1979).[10] In this he proclaims that 'there is no such thing as waste',[11] and goes on to extol the virtues of the composting toilet as a means towards enlightenment both personal and of society in general: 'the smell of hummus is the smell of God, the smell of resurrection, the smell of immortality.'[12]

While Hundertwasser's writings can be seen as a polemic against an aesthetic of architectural cleanliness, control and order, in the light of our expanded understanding they become a prescient and practical blueprint for a positive and informed relationship with the natural world. His work creates an opportunity to rethink the nature of the spaces we inhabit.

Studies of the bacterial make-up of interior spaces have indicated that 'clean' environments are more prone to harbour a far greater number of pathogenic organisms pro rata to the overall bacterial make-up than those of grubbier spaces.[13] The overall microbial loading of the latter is higher, but they are healthier (and likely to be more pleasant) places in which to spend time. Just as the biofilms found in the human appendix are now thought of as repositories of bacteria used to ensure the health of the gut,[14] we can perhaps postulate the design of a similarly functioning microbial 'ark' for the architectural environment.

Not only would this be beneficial for the health of the inhabitants of the space, it would also act as a kind of gazebo, placing the viewer in quite a new place in the natural landscape.

As a starting point for this process, one can consider the historical role of microbes within human culture. The husbandry of yeasts and bacteria has been a commonplace human activity and part of man's relationship with the environment for millennia, a practice that pre-dates the domestication of higher plant and animal species. The production and maturation of wine, cheese and bread all rely upon the actions

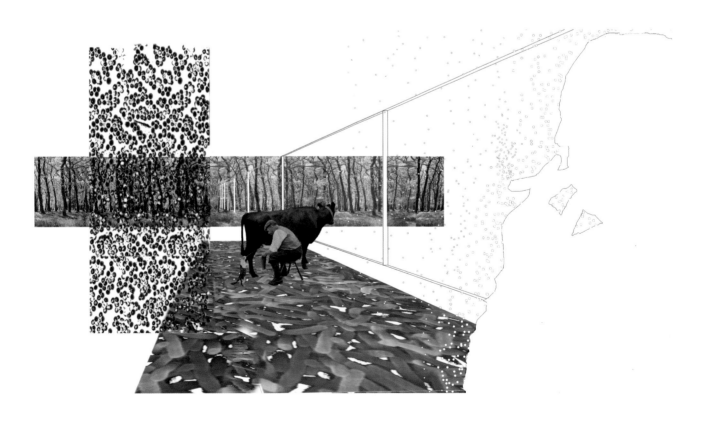

Geoff Ward, Domestic Biome, 2012
Our personal microbiome extends to our local environment, and leaves traces in the air and on surfaces telling of our inhabitation, blurring the boundaries of what is 'us' and what is 'other'. This challenges the notion that our environments can ever really be as minimal and clean as the Modernist dream would have it. Nature, previously regarded at a distance through the security of a glazed screen, is closer (and wilder) than might be comfortably expected.

of microbiological organisms. And quite apart from culinary uses, the exothermic microbial reaction brought on by the decomposition of dung was used by Victorian gardeners to heat greenhouses. The management of bacterial and fungal organisms (in association with, for example, nematodes) in the production of compost is a key activity in the management of waste and synthesis of nutrients and humus to be used in growing plants.

There is a potential for these known and well-understood technologies to be developed and integrated into the current production of spaces to augment and manipulate our biotic surroundings. Encouraging the active involvement of the microbial realm could create environments made up of benign, living components that have the potential to produce an architecture that is aesthetically rich, physiologically healthy and ecologically sound. An architecture able to reframe our relationship with nature neither as one of plunder and subjugation, nor that of romantic distance, but as one able to embrace the natural and engage with the possibilities it has to offer. ᴆ

DEPTH
(MM)

100___

MESOPHILIC PHASE

BACTERIA: 50___
Clostridium
Pseudomonas
Bacillus
Flavobacterium   0___

ACTINOMYCETES:
Streptomyces
                 -50___

FUNGI:
Mucor
Aspergillus
Humicola   -100___

INVERTEBRATES:
Drosophila spp.
(fruit flies)   -150___

                 -200___

THERMOPHILIC PHASE
                 -250___
BACTERIA:
Bacillus
Thermus
                 -300___
ACTINOMYCETES
Streptomyces
Micropolyspora
Thermoactinomycetes -350___
Thermomonospora

FUNGI:
Mucor   -400___
Aspergillus
Humicola
Absidia
Sporotrichum   -450___
Thermoascus

INVERTEBRATES:
Eisena foetida   -500___
(redworms)

                 -550___

                 -600___

HUMIFICATION PHASE

BACTERIA: -650___
Clostridium
Pseudomonas
Bacillus
Flavobacterium   -700___

ACTINOMYCETES:
Streptomyces
                 -800___
FUNGI:
Mucor
Aspergillus
Humicola   -900___

                 -1000___

                 -1050___

Notes

1. Philip and Phylis Morrison, *Powers of Ten*, Scientific American Library (New York), 1982.
2. Jennifer Ackerman, 'The Ultimate Social Network', *Scientific American*, June 2012, pp 21–7.
3. JP Webster, *Rats, Cats, People and Parasites: The Effects of Latent Toxoplasmosis on Behaviour*, University of Oxford, 2001. These alterations of behaviour are claimed to include increasing women's intelligence, decreasing men's intelligence and making both sexes more inclined to self-doubt and insecurity.
4. Mary Douglas, *Purity and Danger: An Analysis of Concepts of Pollution and Taboo*, Routledge (London), 2002.
5. For more on dust, see David Gissen, *Subnature: Architecture's Other Environments*, Princeton Architectural Press (Princeton, NJ), 2009, pp 87–99, and Teresa Stoppani, 'Dust Revelations: Dust, *Informe*, Architecture (Notes for a Reading of Dust in Bataille)', *Journal of Architecture*, Vol 12, No 12, 2007, pp 543–57.
6. Ulrich Conrads, *Programmes and Manifestoes on 20th Century Architecture*, Lund Humphries (London), 1964, pp 157–60.
7. Ibid, p 159.
8. Ibid.
9. Ibid, p 160.
10. Wieland Schmeid, *Hundertwasser: 1928–2000 – Personality, Life, Work*, Taschen (Cologne), 2000, Vol II, pp 949–52.
11. Ibid. p 952.
12. Ibid.
13. Steven W Kembel, Evan Jones, Jeff Kline, Dale Northcutt, Jason Stenson, Ann M Womack, Brendan JM Bohannan, GZ Brown and Jessica L Green, 'Architectural Design Influences the Diversity and Structure of the Built Environment Biome', *The ISME Journal*, No 6, 2012, pp 1469–79.
14. Rob Dunn, *The Wildlife of our Bodies*, HarperCollins (London), 2011, pp 60–110.

Geoff Ward, Compost As Microbial Husbandry, 2012
Composting is an example of the long-established but overlooked relationship that human cultures have held with the microbial realm. The management of decay creates a complex, managed ecosystem that is at one stroke able to dispose of organic waste and simultaneously create fertile humus to raise further crops. With careful management it could additionally be used for carbon-neutral domestic heating.

Nic Clear

Bastian Glaessner, Coalescing Landscape, *The Virtual Palais Idéal,* **film still, Unit 15, Bartlett School of Architecture, University College London (UCL), 2001**
The Virtual Palais Idéal is a sequence of animated digital landscapes created from a variety of 'actual' sources that are then manipulated in a CGI film software to create a strange and sensuous environment that alludes to biological mutation and augmentation.

ARCHITECT, ANIMATOR AND EDUCATOR **NIC CLEAR** CHALLENGES THE CONTEMPORARY NOTION OF THE PASTORAL TO GO BEYOND THE SIMPLISTIC BINARY OPPOSITES OF THE UNTAINTED RURAL IDYLL AND THE INDUSTRIALISED CITY. HE EXPLORES HOW THE NARRATIVES OF THE PASTORAL HAVE PROVIDED A MAINSTAY FOR SCIENCE FICTION AND HOW THIS CAN BE USED TO RE-IMAGINE NATURE ITSELF WITH THE AID OF ADVANCED BIOTECHNOLOGIES TO CREATE NEW ARCHITECTURES FOR THE 21ST CENTURY.

THE PERSISTENCE

The Opening Ceremony of the London 2012 Olympic Games (directed by Danny Boyle) was a spectacular, if somewhat selective, re-imagining of British history and Britishness, and its opening section, titled 'Green and Pleasant Land', offered a perfect example of how the dominant form of the 'pastoral' operates within contemporary culture.

While it was obvious that what was presented was not intended to be historically accurate, the nature of this re-enactment was highly revealing both in the way it manufactured a historical narrative by combining activities, people and events that were clearly from different periods, and in reinforcing popular prejudice regarding the role of the Industrial Revolution in the transformation of the British way of life.

At the very start, the audience was presented with an idyllic rural scene – literally, a 'green and pleasant land' – accompanied by a soundtrack of a single child singing William Blake's 'Jerusalem', and in the surrounding fields people playing cricket and football, dancing around maypoles, and a giant waterwheel gently turning. However, the scene is interrupted by the arrival of a group of men on a fleet of London General Omnibus vehicles dressed predominantly in black, in stark contrast to the white worn by the peasants, and led by a figure that we find out from the programme is Isambard Kingdom Brunel. Brunel surveys the scene before climbing to the top of Glastonbury Tor to read Caliban's 'Be not afeard' speech from Shakespeare's *The Tempest*. In the next section of the ceremony, titled 'Pandemonium', this speech sets in motion the literal tearing up of the countryside, to be replaced by the creation of an industrial landscape, replete with smoking chimneys, where the Olympic rings are forged before their ascent.

This transformation was certainly a spectacular piece of theatre, operating on a level of historical veracity that Fredric Jameson has described as 'pastness',[1] relying on nostalgia and pastiche rather than anything resembling an accurate depiction of events. The narrative it presents of an idyllic pastoral setting being brutally overturned by the onset of a new way of life is exactly the sort of scenario that Raymond Williams depicts in his 1973 book *The Country and the City*, in which he describes the way the pastoral is invariably used as a nostalgic form recalling a previous, more idyllic way of life.[2] Williams traces this tendency back to Ancient Greece[3] and argues that the majority of subsequent versions of the pastoral are used to evoke a previous Golden Age that has been eclipsed by 'the crudeness and narrowness of a new moneyed order'.[4] Significantly, he also contends that from the 18th century onwards, the pastoral begins to assume a depiction of country life explicitly in opposition to the urban.[5]

Williams identifies a number of historical fallacies that surround the pastoral, and there are two in particular that are clearly exemplified by the London 2012 Opening Ceremony. The first concerns the very landscape itself. Williams points out that the form of landscape we most associate with the pastoral, and the one used as the 'green and pleasant land' shown at the start of the opening sequence of the ceremony, is itself a consequence of the processes that were part of the Industrial Revolution, as the landscape had already been transformed as part of a move to industrialised farming and segregated as part of the Enclosure Acts.[6]

The second fallacy is the myth of the happy and smiling 'peasants'; Williams makes extensive references to the hardship and subsistence nature of country life.[7] One of the reasons people fled the countryside was simply to escape the poverty and starvation that was associated with rural life. While living and working conditions in the cities of the Industrial Revolution were no doubt hard, the near serfdom of rural life meant that for many it was a preferable alternative.

The idea of the Industrial Revolution eclipsing an Arcadian version of Albion itself was a strong intellectual theme throughout the late 18th and the 19th century, particularly in the works of social critics from William Blake through to Charles Dickens, and in the Romanticism of William Wordsworth and

amuel Taylor Coleridge. These themes are combined in the
9th century in the writings of John Ruskin and the Arts and
rafts movement with their appeal to the ideals of aestheticism
nd medievalism. Indeed, it could be argued that Ruskin's
ritings in particular have significantly contributed to the idea
hat the Industrial Revolution somehow corrupted and enslaved
he population who had previously been living a simpler and
ore rewarding life.

The 'green and pleasant land' hypothesis has become so
ngrained that it might be considered something that the
istorian Eric Hobsbawm would refer to as 'an invented
adition'.[8] In his book *The Invention of Tradition* (1983),
Hobsbawm identifies a number of cultural narratives, including
he narrative of nationalism itself, that were constructed during
he latter part of the 19th century. The development of the
astoral could be seen as the active re-imagining of Britain
uring the 'Age of Empire'.[9] The idea of an idyllic rural way of
fe being at the heart of the most advanced industrial society,
hich also happened to be the most aggressively expansionist
olonial power at that time, was co-opted by both social
onservatives as part of an ideological narrative to ameliorate the
ns of Empire, and by reformers to suggest an alternative to the
ils of industrial capitalism.

he Pastoral in Science Fiction

here seems an incongruity that the London 2012 Opening
eremony with its pastoral narrative should take place within
ch a 'high-tech' setting, however it should in fact come as no
rprise when one considers that narratives of the pastoral have
en a mainstay for science-fiction and fantasy stories for over a
ntury.

In their canonical *Encyclopedia of Science Fiction* (1993), John
lute and Peter Nicholls offer four main forms of the pastoral
ithin science-fiction literature: the first depicts the invasion
f alien beings into country, or rural, life; the second shows the
se of agricultural and anti-technological societies after some
agined holocaust; the third is set on an alien 'Edenic' or
opian world that is threatened by the intrusion of human or
me form of superior technology; and the fourth is perhaps the
ost straightforward, an escapist adventure set in a simpler, more
imitive environment.[10]

The third form of sci-fi pastoral, the human intrusion into
e utopian alien world, is perhaps most clearly articulated in
rsula K Le Guin's *The Word for World is Forest* (1976),[11] which
agines 19th-century colonialism on a primitive and innocent
anet. Le Guin's description of how an innocent culture is
verthrown by a rampaging technological society was clearly
e inspiration for James Cameron's 2009 film *Avatar*. Although
st known for its use of 3-D special effects, *Avatar* offers a
ear example of a pastoral narrative through the depiction of
e Na'vi, the aboriginal inhabitants of the planet Pandora,
ho live in perfect harmony with their surroundings, being
rt of an ecology that consists of a vast neural network centred
ound the two arboreal motifs of the 'Hometree' and the 'Tree
Souls'.[12] The Na'vi way of life is threatened by the rampant
dustrialisation of alien humans in search of the mineral
nobtanium'.

Avatar is currently ranked as the highest grossing film of
l time.[13] In another major film franchise, Peter Jackson's *The*

IN POPULAR VERSIONS OF
THE PASTORAL, NATURE IS
REPRESENTED AS BENIGN
AND MORALLY SUPERIOR TO
TECHNOLOGY, A DICHOTOMY
THAT IS IS PERFECTLY
ENCAPSULATED IN THE 'CITY
VERSUS COUNTRY' DEBATE.

Lord of the Rings trilogy (2001–03) based upon the book by JRR
Tolkien (written between 1937 and 1949),[14] also has a pastoral
motif at the centre of the narratives. In both book and film,
the pastoral shires of Middle Earth are juxtaposed against the
demonic industrialised city of Mordor. Both *Avatar* and *The Lord
of the Rings* perpetuate the opposition of technology and nature,
and city and country, where technology and city are always bad
and nature is always good.

Perhaps one of the most unusual intersections of the pastoral,
science fiction, social critique and utopian manifesto is William
Morris's *News from Nowhere* (1890).[15] One of the leading figures
in the Arts and Crafts movement and a key influence on Tolkien,
Morris presents a future vision of London as a medieval pastoral
and socialist utopia.

Synthetic Natures

In popular versions of the pastoral, nature is represented
as benign and morally superior to technology, a dichotomy
that is is perfectly encapsulated in the 'city versus country'
debate. However, such a simplistic binary opposition is clearly
outmoded, and we need to ask what are the possible models of
the pastoral given the changes in our understanding of nature
itself?

While the use of nature in the pastoral has always assumed
that it is nature cultivated by human society and organised
and manipulated by human agency, the development of fully
synthetic natures through the techniques of DNA sequencing
and genetic modification, nanotechnology, protocell technology,
wet computing, and the plethora of artificial ecologies and
organisms question what we actually mean by nature. The form
of these advances often blurs the very line between nature and
technology, and science and science fiction.

If our understanding of nature is being transformed by
these new technologies, then how might they impact on our
understanding of the pastoral? And how might we begin to
develop a whole strand of new architectures that are facilitated as
a result of these new technologies?

Since 1998, the postgraduate design Unit 15, first at the
Bartlett School of Architecture, University College London
(UCL) and since 2011 at the University of Greenwich, has
specialised in the use of film, animation and motion graphics
to generate, develop and represent architectural projects. One
of the key themes of the design teaching here is to encourage
students to develop architectures predicated on the use of

Dan Tassell, Synthetic Arboretum, *The Battersea Experiment,* film still, Unit 15, Bartlett School of Architecture, UCL, 2010
Battersea Power Station is transformed through the use of self-organising living technologies to create a network of surrealist interfaces that allow for cultural exchange between man, technology and nature.

KIBWE TAVARES'S AWARD-WINNING FILM *ROBOTS OF BRIXTON* ... IMAGINES THE INHABITANTS OF BRIXTON AS ARTIFICIAL INTELLIGENCES (AIS) WHO HAVE BECOME THE 'UNDERCLASS' OF A FUTURE DYSTOPIA.

Keiichi Matsuda, Ministry of Abundance, Technocratic Retrofit of London, Unit 15, Bartlett School of Architecture, UCL, 2009
Section perspective. The Ministry of Abundance is the central manifestation of a post-capitalist programme to re-imagine the City of London using advanced high-yield bio-intensive agriculture as a self-sufficient entity. The shift in political and economic systems results in new values and new meanings within the city itself.

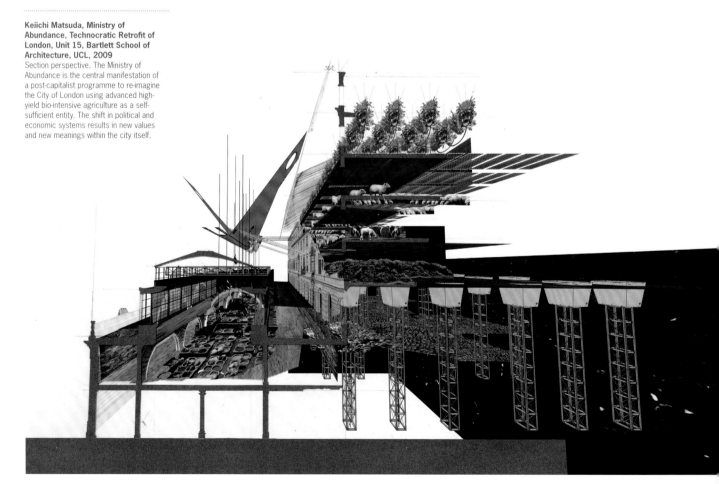

vanced technology, and particularly nano-, bio-, info- and cogno- (NBIC) technologies.[16] The use of these technologies, often driven by narratives derived from science fiction, can offer students the opportunity to imagine a future of architecture free from the constraints of the profession and the restrictions of cost and patronage and, in conjunction with the moving image, do so in a way that makes those ideas palpable to a non-professional audience.[17]

Many of the student projects that have been developed as part of both iterations of Unit 15 represent a range of positions from coherently developed extrapolations of existing technologies, allegorical social critiques of race and class, through to musings on subjectivity and agency where 'life' becomes an abstracted hybrid of organism and environment.

There are perhaps three types of student project that deal with these ideas. First are those that push existing technologies, often to their limits, such as Dan Tassell's Battersea Experiment where living technologies are first used to stabilise the existing fabric of Sir Giles Gilbert Scott's Battersea Power Station in London, and then developed to create a lush symbiotic self-organising ecology that takes over the whole space, in a manner that is informed by JG Ballard's *The Crystal World* (1966).[18] As part of the development of the project, Tassell employed virtual models to 'grow' the infrastructures over an extended period of time.

Another example would be Keiichi Matsuda's Technocratic retrofit of London where a City of London abandoned by the financiers becomes the site of a new independent technocratic community that utilises high-yield bio-intensive agriculture, powered by tethered aerostats, and imagined to be entirely self-sufficient.

A third and very different example is Kibwe Tavares's award-winning film *Robots of Brixton*, in which he imagines the inhabitants of Brixton as artificial intelligences (AIs) who have become the 'underclass' of a future dystopia. In the middle section of the film, the AIs retreat into their own private world, a synthetic forest echoing both the forms of Marc-Antoine (Abbé) Laugier's 'primitive hut' (1755) and the grandeur of a Gothic cathedral. This idyllic interlude is rudely interrupted by an outbreak of social violence from the physical space of the city as the AIs battle their oppressors. Tavares's film controversially received the RIBA Silver Medal, perhaps because it so presciently foresaw the UK's summer riots of 2011; it less controversially won a special animation award at the Sundance Film Festival because it is an outstanding piece of filmmaking.

The second type of project relies more on positing a 'possible' technology as the basis of an architectural idea. Many of these take Ray Kurzweil's hypothesis of 'Singularity' as their starting point,[19] and particularly the conception of 'foglets', a form of nano-tech programmable matter. Paul Nicholls's Golden Age Interiors used foglet technology to create evolving landscapes where an interior can literally morph into a series of pre-programmed forms, often imitating 'natural' environments. Richard Hardy, in his Transcendent City, develops an even more extreme scenario where human and artificial intelligences combine and form a symbiotic relationship with the natural environment to create a 'transcendent' meta-system engineered at the molecular scale through self-organising programmable matter controlled by nano-scale molecular computers. According

Kibwe Tavares, Virtual Robot Interior, *Robots of Brixton*, film stills, Unit 15, Bartlett School of Architecture, UCL, 2010
Robots of Brixton projects contemporary issues of race and class into a future London where artificial intelligences (AIs) occupy the lowest and most menial roles of society. In this section, the robots move into their own virtual landscape, a world of artificial nature consciously referencing Marc-Antoine (Abbé) Laugier's description of the 'primitive hut' as the origin of architectural form in the second edition of his famous 'Essay on Architecture' in 1755.

Lucas Tizard, Posthuman Merger, *Prosthetic Environments*, film still, Unit 15, Bartlett School of Architecture, UCL, 2009
bottom: *Prosthetic Environments* depicts a synthetic landscape where the boundary between man, technology and nature is blurred and the form of the post-human becomes an augmented biomechanical hybrid, an extension of both physical and virtual spaces actualised through intelligent self-organising networks.

Richard Hardy, *The Transcendent City*, film still, Unit 15, Bartlett School of Architecture, UCL, 2010
top: *The Transcendent City* is a future city where artificial intelligence (AI) has created an ecosystem through the manipulation of nano-technologies and molecular computing to create an environment that, though constantly evolving, exists in a state of homeostasis.

Paul Nicholls, *The Golden Age Part 2*, film still, Unit 15, Bartlett School of Architecture, UCL, 2010
centre: In future architectures, the building fabric will be constructed from programmable matter or 'foglets', allowing the creation of endlessly variable environments that are able to morph into a bewildering possibility of options emulating almost any type of system. Here, the interior of an apartment becomes a lush park.

WHAT IS EXCITING ABOUT THESE PROJECTS IS THE WAY THEY TRANSCEND DISCIPLINES, COMBINING SPATIAL DESIGN, ADVANCED TECHNOLOGY, CYBERNETICS, HYBRID ECOLOGIES AND VIRTUALITY

Hardy: 'the project questions whether artificial intelligence has been a teleological necessity in human evolution and we should therefore embrace emergent technologies to engage with problems of sustainability and the city'.[20]

The third and perhaps most extreme form of project are propositions for completely virtual landscapes. These projects move beyond the assumption that architecture is bound by physical space, and explore architectural scenarios engendered by fully immersive technologies. Bastian Glaessner's *Virtual Palais Idéal* was formed through a process of digitally manipulating scans of biological matter and then digitally painting and animating these to create a strange environment of coalescing forms. The resultant landscape combines the spatial multiplicities of the baroque with the smeared abstract paintings of Gerhard Richter. Glaessner has gone on to direct music videos for artists including Björk as part of the Lynn Fox directing group.

In *Prosthetic Environments*, Lucas Tizard imagines an landscape where the boundaries between the human, the mechanical and the virtual are broken down to create a hyper trans-humanism. The film deliberately sets up an ambiguous relationship where it is impossible to tell whether the human form is augmented by the virtual and technological prosthesis, or whether it is the virtual landscape that is augmented by the human and the mechanical. The final project was developed as a multi-screen environment that completely immersed viewers in the synthetic space of these bio-mechanical virtual hybrids.

While these projects seek to utilise and develop architectural propositions in very different ways, they share one critical point of departure – they are all looking forward, trying to deal creatively with how new technologies might redefine our ideas of nature, and thereby transform our ideas of the pastoral. From pedagogical position, what is exciting about these projects is the way they transcend disciplines, combining spatial design, advanced technology, cybernetics, hybrid ecologies and virtuality opening up possibilities of what architecture might be rather than simply relying on what it is and what it was.

New Pastoralism: Nature Re-Imagined

The pastoral can be seen to persist on two levels: first as it has done since the 18th century, through nostalgia and pastiche exemplified by the London 2012 Opening Ceremony. This mainstream use of the pastoral as an idealised version of nature is clearly fictional, but despite its fictive status it is a persistent and attractive fiction; its persistence is perhaps due to the utilisation of a simplified and outmoded version of nature presented as an image. This tendency to reduce to an image echoes the way that mainstream culture deals with technology itself, as an image, and usually an outmoded image of machinic technology.

However, the pastoral can also be said to persist at a much more significant level, as a re-imagining of nature itself, a questioning of what nature actually is, and how intelligent systems might manipulate it to create architectures of the 21st century. The forms that these new natures might take can only be developed through a speculative engagement that looks forward, a shift in emphasis that architecture itself must undergo, to stop dealing with what was and look to the future to create what might be. ⌂

Notes
1. Frederic Jameson, 'Postmodernism, or The Cultural Logic of Late Capitalism', *New Left Review* I/146, July/August 1984, p 67.
2. Raymond Williams, *The Country and the City*, Paladin (St Albans), 1973.
3. Ibid, pp 23–31.
4. Ibid, p 49.
5. Ibid, pp 61–71.
6. Ibid, pp 121–34.
7. Ibid, pp 221–38.
8. Eric Hobsbawm and Terence Ranger (eds), *The Invention of Tradition*, Cambridge University Press (Cambridge), 1983.
9. Eric Hobsbawm, *The Age of Empire: 1875–1914*, Weidenfeld and Nicolson, (London), 1987.
10. John Clute and Peter Nicholls, *The Encyclopedia of Science Fiction*, Orbit (London), 1993, p 915.
11. Ursula K Le Guin, *The Word for World is Forest*, Putnam Publishing Group (New York), 1976.
12. This use of the arboreal motif is reminiscent of one of the most ingrained founding narratives of architecture, Marc-Antoine (Abbé) Laugier's 'primitive hut', where nature in the form of a cluster of trees is literally formed by Mother Architecture to create the first dwelling. See Joseph Rykwert, *On Adam's House in Paradise: The Idea of the Primitive Hut in Architectural History*, Museum of Modern Art (New York), 1972, pp 43–50.
13. All Time Worldwide Box Office Grosses: www.boxofficemojo.com/alltime/world, accessed 1 October 2012.
14. *The Lord of the Rings: The Fellowship of the Ring*, 2001; *The Two Towers*, 2002; *The Return of the King*, 2003, adapted from JRR Tolkien, *The Lord of the Rings* and *The Two Towers*, both George Allen and Unwin (London), 1954, and *The Return of the King*, George Allen and Unwin (London), 1955.
15. William Morris, *News from Nowhere, Or, An Epoch of Rest: Being Some Chapters from a Utopian Romance*, Longmans, Green & Co (London), 1908.
16. This is also the main thrust of the Advanced Virtual and Technological Architectural Research (AVATAR) group founded by Professor Neil Spiller, of which the author is a director. AVATAR's multidisciplinary research involves biologists, chemists, engineers and philosophers, as well as architects and designers.
17. These projects have largely been developed as part of the final Diploma/MArch Thesis with students already having addressed the majority of the ARB/RIBA technical and professional criteria in the first year of their postgraduate studies.
18. JG Ballard, *The Crystal World*, Jonathan Cape (London), 1966.
19. Ray Kurzweil, *The Singularity is Near: When Humans Transcend Biology*, Viking, (New York), 2005.
20. Richard Hardy, in Nic Clear (ed), *Unit 15 New Works 2008–2009*, Bartlett School of Architecture (London), 2009.

LANDSCAPE UTOPIANISM

INFORMATION, ECOLOGY AND GENERATIVE PASTORALISM

Architect and educator **Gregory Marinic** describes how the 21st century is witnessing the rise of a new utopianism through landscape/architectural interventions that pursue the possibilities of 'ersatz utopias within our quotidian world'. He illustrates this with his own collaborative works and competition entries for d3, an art-architecture stewardship programme based in New York of which he is director.

Arquipelago (Gregory Marinic and Kevin Pham) and Megapixelstudios (Meg Jackson), Coastal Harvest, Ann Arbor, Michigan, USA, 'Sukkah Arbor' competition, 2012
This project received a Design-Build Award and employs emergent design processes derived from cultural, ecological and structural inquiries. Makers of the sukkah annually participate in mitigating an invasive species impacting shorelines in the Great Lakes region of North America.

… whereas nature, like a kind parent, hath freely given us the best things, such as air, earth, and water, but hath hidden from us those which are vain and useless.
— Thomas More, *Utopia*, Book 2, *c* 1516

[U]topianism is a concept that has undergone [co]ntinual transformation throughout time. [Fo]r Thomas More – an English lawyer, social [ph]ilosopher, Renaissance humanist and Roman [Ca]tholic saint – coined the term 'utopia' in [15]16 to embody his vision of an ideal and [im]aginary island. More described progressive [po]litical arrangements and social organisations [th]at significantly contrasted with the ongoing [wa]rfare and upheaval endemic to medieval [Eu]ropean states. In his *Utopia*, communal [lan]d ownership, gender equality and religious [to]lerance stood in marked contrast to reality. [Ba]sed on monastic communalism, he traced its [ori]gins to the Greek words for 'no place' ('*ou [top]os*') and 'good place' ('*eu topos*'). Since its [inc]eption, this ambiguous 'place' has remained [a r]ealm of inquiry for theorists, philosophers, [his]torians and architects.

By the 20th century, utopian thought [ha]d become thoroughly embedded within [th]e social promise of modern architecture.[1] [Ut]opia shifted from a conceptual 'nowhere' [in] the minds of philosophers, and became ['so]mewhere' in the fantastical ponderings of architects. The celestial became terrestrial; the abstractions of philosophy, literature and art became increasingly worldly. In the East, Kasimir Malevich's utopian towns, Mikhail Okhitovich's patterned collectives, Frederick Kiesler's space settlements and Georgii Krutikov's flying cities offered the most avant-garde Suprematist projections of this future. In the West, Le Corbusier's urban projects from the 1920s and 1930s clearly reflected this 'heroic' phase of Modernism, while his desires for 'sun control' and 'exact air' assumed a stunningly human-controlled future for even the most fundamental aspects of ecology.[2]

In the years that followed, these sensational visions of the future came to be viewed as pure utopian fantasies. By the early 1980s, the Modernist social experiment had been tarnished and utopianism was subsequently declared dead by leading theorists. In their co-authored classic *Collage City* (1984), Colin Rowe and Fred Koetter claimed that the second half of the 20th century represented utopia's final 'decline and fall'.[3] For Rowe and Koetter, its demise was voiced with a profound sense of regret. Since that time, we have been living in an increasingly anti-utopian age. Under what type of conditions would the re-imagination of utopian futures become possible? From the standpoint of architecture, the millennial rise of digital processes and ecological imperatives signals a renewed interest in and expectation for the utopian project.

Representing a concept or place that is not real but implies perfection, the contemporary relevance of utopianism has increasingly shifted away from the unattainable social projections of the future and towards the potential for ersatz utopias within our quotidian world. In 1967, philosopher Michel Foucault employed the term 'heterotopia' to describe such places and spaces that blend multifaceted layers of meaning, as well as connectivity to other places.[4] These worlds of otherness, which are neither here nor there, engage physical, mental and phenomenological characteristics. Thus, by appropriating aspects of idealism, heterotopias represent a physical manifestation and approximation of utopia among a shared people. This essay casts its lens on the recent rise of utopian-heterotopian influences in pastoralism, as well as the impact of generative emergence within current architectural discourse. It surveys various endeavours that position, embrace, blur and promote generative approaches to blending buildings with landscapes.

Generative Duality

Based within the discipline of human geography, Foucault describes places and spaces that function as non-hegemonic systems.[5] Using

[Ar]quipelago (Gregory Marinic, Nicolas [Her]rera and Kevin Pham), Botanis [Can]adensis, Winnipeg, Manitoba, Canada, ['Wa]rming Huts' competition, 2013
[bel]ow: Employing a generative design process [deri]ved from the taxonomic blending of [bio]logical information, this proposal for the ['Wa]rming Huts' 2013 competition uses a [bott]om-up, generative methodology. Form was [foun]d rather than prescribed.

natural materials / natural dyes / natural processes / natural space

a mirror as a metaphor for real–unreal dualities and contradictions, he alludes to utopianism by engaging an image that does not physically exist. Furthermore, he suggests a broader view into the more commonplace and everyday concept of utopianism – or heterotopianism – since the mirror is an object that reshapes the view of oneself.[6] The complexity of a digitally driven design culture assumes a similar relationship to the surreal multiplicity that Foucault proposes. Heterotopias function in relation to illusion by creating physical environments that expose the limitations of the ordinary and opportunities for otherness. From an ecological perspective, the recent interest in pastoral, hybridised landscape/architectural interventions suggests a shifting view of heterotopia. These new experiments allude to potentially 'real' places that incorporate landscape microcosms of highly speculative pastoral built environments.

Since the turn of the millennium, there has been a discernible change in the way that landscape has been influenced by utopianism. An impressive wave of visionary design competitions has given rise to a parallel universe of virtual realities that contribute to a growing digital archive of landscape interventions. Super-tall skyscrapers, off-grid infrastructures, vertical farms, dystopian transformations and artificial islands offer wildly experimental

new geographies that recast our collective expectations of how architecture might more fluidly blend with landscape. Suggesting an alternative future, these contemporary landscape utopias radicalise our hopes and anxieties of a future world that integrates a more blurred relationship between buildings and natural ecologies. As such, the most recent experimentations reveal an interest in visionary architecture that engages nature as the ultimate utopian project.

What are the expectations of utopia in the 21st century? How does the current notion of pastoral utopianism, and its understanding of landscape, differ from previous eras? The recent emergence of pastoralism in architecture compels architects to activate elements of Romanticism filtered by ecology. Identifying nature as an amenity, pastoralism and its inherently low-tech tradition builds upon the timeless notion that nature offers delight. Thus, the approach blends landscape with form, culture and technology to assume highly variant responses to global-local vernacular conditions.

From Control to Emergence

If architecture is a living organism that should be given the opportunity to emerge from fluid conceptual processes, pastoral opportunities leverage this methodology with contextual, environmental and ecological potentials. Recent

shifts in sustainable discourse have allowed the design process to become increasingly aware of ecology, while offering vast procedural complexity. In an era characterised by economic instability and environmental degradation, architects find great solace in the romantic appeal of an idealised landscape. With the rise of ecological imperatives, they increasingly identify performatively informed alternatives that simultaneously test, critique and interrogate conventional approaches to the pastoral world. These issues assume a need to radically reconsider various normative conditions.

Emerging 21st-century needs are replacing the conventional hierarchical parameters of optimisation, control, predictability and clarity. Responding with reframed methodologies, designers are engaging generatively derived ecological, cultural and geographic factors. How can interdisciplinary design practice mitigate the historically contentious territories of architecture, landscape, urbanism and ecology into a more integrated design practice?

Under the guise of sustainability, it may be argued that the potential for an expanded environmental relevance has been increasingly seized by a limiting agenda of 'enlightened practice'. Such practices often reduce architecture to generic and place-

Liminal Projects (Omar Khan, Laura Garofalo, A Mathur and T Pydipally), Home Spun, d3 'Housing Tomorrow' competition, 2010
Home Spun received first prize in the d3 'Housing Tomorrow' 2010 competition. It proposes an environmentally tuned infill housing concept for shrinking cities in the Great Lakes region of North America.

There are no restrictions on site, scale, programme or building typology, though proposals should carefully address their selected context.

elevant standards, operational concerns
d construction efficiencies. Designers are
lf-organising and mobilising to reposition
ology without the burden of what
stainability now implies. Responding to
ese issues, this essay asserts that generative
ocesses and technological advances allow
ildings to activate social flows, material
haviours, cultural relevance and formal
rformance through an ecological lens. While
rly emergent inquiries in the 1990s focused
computational processes for finding and
stifying form, recent shifts illustrate that
ergence has migrated beyond mere dualisms.
he exemplars featured here illustrate recent
chitectural interventions assuming a more
mantic view of landscape. These projects are
nditioned with place-based cultural relevance,
well as blended architectures that continually
olve with social, ecological and performative
mplexities.

rformative Pastoralism

he rise in pastoral inquiries blends
manticism with a multilayered awareness
, and expectation for, performance.
rformativity may be described in spatial
nditions experienced in our everyday lives.
linguistic terms, the word is derived from
e root designation 'performative'. English
ilosopher John Langshaw Austin defined

'performative' as something that goes beyond
simply describing the world. Rather, he
asserts that it participates in actively changing
something.[7] Critiquing Austin's notion of
the performative, Jacques Derrida valued the
distinctiveness of each speech act, since it places
a specific effect in the particular situation where
it is performed.[8] Derrida's early postulations
lend support to the notion of design emergence:

> The performative does not describe
> something that exists outside of language
> and prior to it. It produces or transforms a
> situation, it effects.[9]

Derrida's concept can be transposed from
linguistics into the shaping of architecture,
space and objects. Thus, we may assume that
aspects of our material culture need not simply
occupy space as mute and inert entities. Rather,
their performativity offers the potential to act
upon us and our everyday lives. Critiquing
Austin's view that context is vital to the efficacy
of a performative utterance, Derrida notes:

> Context is never absolutely determinable.[10]

It may be argued that performativity is a
characteristic of all objects designed to interact
with the human condition. While their
performative qualities may not be intentionally

designed, performance is inherent to the
nature of objects, as well as spaces and places
that engage human activities. Thus, contextual
contingencies offer a more objective first path
towards the performative approach in the
design process. Awareness of performance
supports emergence; it assumes that form is
an outgrowth of layered inquiries.
Significant interest in the notion of design
emergence has developed within architectural
discourse. The emergent approach employs
design research focusing on generative
form-finding techniques that guide the
performative and behavioural aspects of
building form. Beyond architecture, the
current interest in emergence within the
natural sciences may suggest the need to
provide a scientific explanation of the trend.
John H Holland explains the concept of
emergence as a simple theory that supports
that the whole is greater than the sum of
its parts. From this standpoint, emergence
demonstrates that a core set of rules or laws
can generate incredibly complex systems.[11]
Thus, a fertilised egg can programme the
entire development of a human being, while
closer to architectural principles, ants work
collaboratively towards a shared goal of colony
building. For Holland, emergence is a journey
through rules and behaviours beginning with
simplicity and migrating towards complexity.

uipelago (Gregory Marinic and Nicolas Herrera) and
brose&Sabatino (Michelangelo Sabatino), Sukkanoe,
onto, Canada, 'Sukkaville Toronto' competition, 2012
ner of a Design-Build Award, the project employs generative
ign processes derived from blended spiritual and material
ctices, and forms part of the permanent collection of the
adian Canoe Museum.

**Boulos Douaihy, Grow, d3 'Housing Tomorrow'
competition, 2010**
Receiving a special mention, this submission
proposes a medium-density, clustered residential
alternative to conventional suburban development.

The simultaneous rise in pastoral influences challenges singularity by reinvesting complexity within the utopian allure of landscape.

Following similar principles, Steven Johnson's popular book *Emergence* summarises the concept as a transition from low-level rule sets to high levels of sophistication.[12]

Promoting Emergence

Founded in New York in 2008, the d3 art-architecture-design stewardship organisation was conceived to promote, support and document the development of emergence and transdisciplinary design practices within architecture. It develops speculative programmes for architects, designers, artists and students worldwide. Identifying synergies between design practice, mass media, popular culture and the avant-garde, the organisation works to provide a collaborative framework for creative experimentation through exhibitions, events, competitions and publications that generate worldwide dialogue across geographic, ideological and disciplinary boundaries in art, design and the built environment.

In 2009, d3 established the annual 'Natural Systems' and 'Housing Tomorrow' competitions that invite architects, designers, engineers and students worldwide to collectively explore the potential of emergence and nature-based influences in architecture, interiors and designed objects. Annual competitions solicit innovative proposals that advance sustainable thought and performance through the study of

intrinsic environmental geometries, behaviour and flows. By examining and applying their structural order on form and function, new solutions for limitless building typologies, functional programmes and material condition are realised.

Emergent architecture suggests that desig expression requires purpose beyond formal assumption and aesthetic experimentation alone. Concurrent with sustainable thought, d3 competitions assume that architecture does not simply form, but rather performs various functions beyond those conventionally associa with buildings. Thus, exploring microscopic to universal natural systems reveals vast potentia for alternative architectonic strategies that leverage this potential conceptually. Submissio must be environmentally responsible, while advancing innovative conceptual solutions. Although proposals should be technologically feasible, they may also suggest fantastical architectural visions of a sustainable global future. As these are open competitions, design have the freedom to approach their creative processes in a scale-appropriate manner – fro large-scale masterplanning endeavours to individual building concepts and notions of interior detail. There are no restrictions on sit scale, programme or building typology, thoug proposals should carefully address their select context.

d3 believes that enlightened design practice participates in a common charge to design and create a better world. Since its inception, its competitions have grown, evolved and migrated to reveal rapid transformations within design practice and academia. As worldwide forums, 'Natural Systems' and 'Housing Tomorrow' offer a window onto progressive practices that are actively shifting the way architects, designers and students approach their craft. Competition submissions participate in a self-initiated, bottom-up effort that collectively extends this goal. In doing so, built form is positioned to reflect its time; with care and complexity of a design process that speculates on the impact of shifting challenges, subtle changes may be discerned on an annual basis.

Identifying a further need to define a platform for unbuilt, visionary and, thus, utopian design projects, in 2012 d3 initiated the 'Unbuilt Visions' competition-exhibition programme. 'Unbuilt Visions' has received considerable worldwide appeal. Collecting work from annual worldwide calls, d3 competition submissions represent an exceptional array of design speculation at the highest conceptual and graphic levels of quality. Together, submitted works reveal the dramatic shifts that continually transform tools, techniques and aesthetic within experimental architectural visualisation on a global scale.

Reflecting

The idea that the future will be better than the present is not new. However, the way in which it is perceived has shifted towards a natural paradigm, and it may therefore be argued that the 21st century has witnessed utopia in transition. Emerging from the austere cocoon of late-1990s Neo-Minimalism, and offering a ground-up platform for emergence, a proliferation of recent speculative work reinterprets the role of the pastoral in architecture. Increased awareness of the complexities found in nature has paralleled a renewed interest in fluidity, ornament, pattern making and performance, as well as cultural ideals and humanist implications of pastoral architecture. The most avant-garde and experimental of these projects have rattled the core presumptions of conservative critics, while more simple responses signal a return to the low-tech. The simultaneous rise in pastoral influences challenges singularity by reinvesting complexity within the utopian allure of landscape. Here, ecological performance and cultural context act as the primary shapers of a utopian vision of the future. ∆

Notes

1. Manfredo Tafuri, *Architecture and Utopia: Design and Capitalist Development*, MIT Press (Cambridge, MA), 1976, pp 136–7. Tafuri's critique represents an early challenge to the Deconstructivist perspective that dominated the social sciences in the late 1960s and 1970s.
2. Le Corbusier, *The Radiant City: Elements of a Doctrine of Urbanism to be Used as the Basis of Our Machine-Age Civilization*, Paris, 1933, p 42.
3. Colin Rowe and Fred Koetter, *Collage City*, MIT Press (Cambridge, MA), 1984, pp 9-31.
4. Michel Foucault, 'Of Other Spaces (Heterotopias)', 1967. This text, originally entitled 'Des espaces autres', and published by the French journal of architectural theory *Architecture/Mouvement/Continuité* in October 1984, was given as a lecture by Foucault in March 1967. The manuscript was released into the public domain for an exhibition in Berlin shortly before Foucault's death.
5. Ibid.
6. Ibid.
7. John Langshaw Austin, *How to Do Things with Words*, Oxford University Press (Oxford), 1976.
8. Jacques Derrida, 'Signature Event Context', in Alan Bass (trans), *Margins of Philosophy*, University of Chicago Press (Chicago, IL), 1985.
9. Ibid.
10. Ibid.
11. John H Holland, *Emergence: From Chaos to Order*, Basic Books (New York), 1999, p 3.
12. Steven Johnson, *Emergence: The Connected Lives of Ants, Brains, Cities, and Software*, Scribner (New York), 2001, p 18.

Forest Fulton Architecture, Lace Hill, d3 'Housing Tomorrow' competition, 2011
opposite: Lace Hill radically rethinks housing strategies for Yerevan, the capital of Armenia. It received second prize in the d3 'Housing Tomorrow' 2011 competition.

Insung Son, Sinwoo Lee, Yoonseok Hwang, Eunji Lee and Bora Kim, Green Earth Worm, d3 'Natural Systems', 2012
below: This submission to d3 'Natural Systems' 2012 received a special mention. It proposes a landscape-based communal live-work environment.

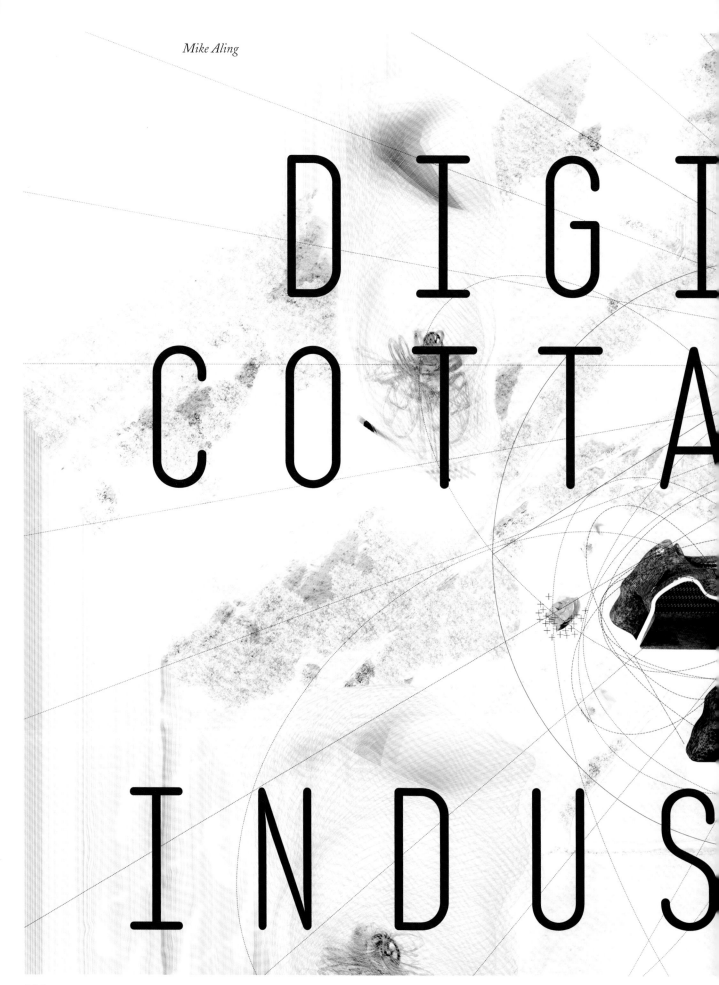

Mike Aling

DIGI
COTTA

INDUS

TAL
GE
G E

TRIES

Mike Aling, Prounstretcher MMVIII, After *Sleep Furiously*, 2012
A monolith as mobile library, towed into (one of a number of) position(s) across the remote mid-Wales landscape by night. Sited in the isolated landscape of Gideon Koppel's *Sleep Furiously* (2008), the architecture sits ominously while the accompanying aerial radially emits hypersonic frequencies to attract local residents and committed readers/library members from remote locations. As both public libraries and the print industry continue into terminal decline, the monolith allows for physical books to be pre-ordered online and grown in a portable nano-vat while visitors pass the time inside the oily darkness of the interior, singing in a phantom choir of distant neighbours' recorded voices (this then transmitted via hypersonic sound). Meanwhile, a self-propelling sack race orbits outside, a requiem for the number of school buildings recently closed in the area.

Mike Aling's ProunStretcher project engages with the recent global revival of cottage industries, fuelled by the application of digital technologies, as a means to address 'the manifold social issues present across our rural landscape-as-urban-extension'.

A global renaissance in cottage industries is currently underway, fuelled by a wide spectrum of digital communications – from smart phones to the Internet and, increasingly, the technologies of virtuality (ranging from augmented reality to fully immersive virtual reality). A growing number of products – digital or otherwise – floating on the pervasive cybermarket are being developed and distributed from the home. This re-emerging para-industry, global in scale and regional in consequence, subsumes many sectors using digital avenues as sales and marketing vehicles, from mohair products in Ireland[1] to curios upcycled from washed-up flip-flops in Kenya[2] and the scanning of literature to generate ebooks in Japan.[3] Up until the digital age, cottage industries were located on sites disconnected from industrial and urban centres. Today, however, following William Gibson's recent identification of the 'ageographical and largely unrecognized meta city that is the Internet',[4] it is increasingly difficult to identify spaces that are outside of the urban process.

With the city/country antinomy ever blurring (a dialectic that the city has come to dominate), the Digital Cottage Industries project concentrates on the rural side of the blur as a site for small-scale cottage-industry architectures in the UK. Where certain areas of the British countryside can often be targeted critically as a space for the hubristic pursuits of the well-to-do urban self-exile, this project advocates various advanced technologies (such as augmented reality, developments in stereoscopic camera mapping, hypersonic sound and nanotechnology) as a mechanism to engage with the manifold social issues present across our rural landscape-as-urban-extension. These range from the erosion of rural communities and erasure of public services to contested land ownership and public access rights. If the countryside will continue to be an increasingly exercised zone for cyber-industry, then Henri Lefebvre's 'right to the city', classified by Jacob Emery as the public 'right to command the whole urban process, which … increasingly dominat[es] the countryside through phenomena ranging from agribusiness to second homes and rural tourism'[5] (the city now encompassing both the actual and virtual/meta city), will become increasingly prevalent across the British landscape and will require a meme in which to develop.

With the city/country antinomy ever blurring (a dialectic that the city has come to dominate), the Digital Cottage Industries project concentrates on the rural side of the blur as a site for small-scale cottage-industry architectures in the UK.

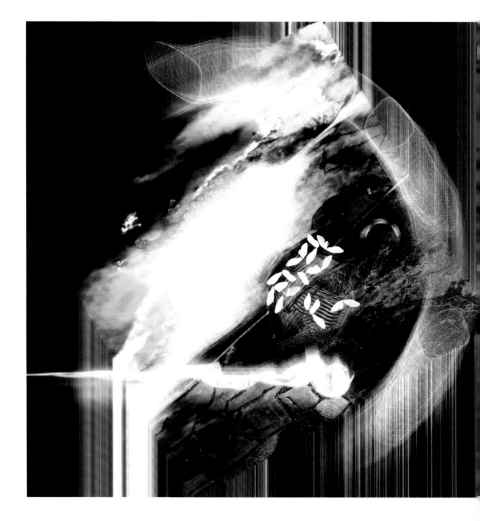

Mike Aling, Prounstretcher MCMLXXI, After *Straw Dogs*, 2012
Home for a virtual learning tutor in Cornwall specialising in prisoner education. Situated in the landscape of Sam Peckinpah's *Straw Dogs* (1971), a coastal site with ever-turbulent changes in weather, the teaching workplace is a virtuality continuum 'portico' sited next to the home, set for two-way augmented transmission into Her Majesty's Prison Service.

yspastoral Cinema

The truth of the vision of nature lies in the way in which it discloses the complacency of the urban celebration; but the opposite is also true, and the vision of the city exposes everything nostalgic and impoverished in the embrace of nature.
— Fredric Jameson (2004)[6]

Cinema represents landscape in a way that no other edia can. The cinematic lens has acclimatised our viewing films to one of continual motion, and it is perhaps the lative stillness of the natural landscape that often comes cross as extremely powerful. The pastoral vision of the itish countryside perpetuated by cinema has largely been means of setting historical narratives, of which there is long list of costume dramas. However, when it comes to lising rural environments for contemporary narratives, e number of films decreases enormously. Furthermore, storal-futurology is surprisingly nonexistent in cinema, and e future is largely depicted through urban environments. e have to look back to late-19th-century literature to find storal utopia narratives by socialist writers such as William enry Hudson (*A Crystal Age*, 1887), William Morris (*News om Nowhere,* 1890) and William Dean Howells (*A Traveler om Altruria*, 1894).

There have been a select number of British independent ns produced since the Second World War that film theorist eter Hutchings describes as 'anti-landscape' cinema, films at relish in the 'dyspastoral'[7] as a means of allegorising the er-challenging urban condition:

[Cinema that] might best be thought of as the British anti-landscape, the landscape that provocatively throws into question the very idea of the human/national subject as the owner of landscape, as a figure in that landscape, or as an observer of it.[8]

Set in the present day, recent films such as Duane Hopkins's *Better Things* (2008), Marek Losey's *The Hide* (2008) and Gideon Koppel's *Sleep Furiously* (2008) indicate a resurgence of dyspastoral themes in British independent cinema. These films have a number of antecedents, many of which are chosen as sites for the architectures in the Digital Cottage Industries project.[9] These dyspastoral films have quite possibly garnered an audience due to the recent recession, fuelled by an increasing fervour of distrust towards the finance sector and other negative attributes associated with the late capitalist urban process. Cinematic representations of the countryside as an alien, bewildering and untrustworthy environment seem to indicate how disorientating the urban experience has become for many, the rural setting in this situation becoming a somewhat melancholic heterotopia reflecting a sense of loss in urbanite ambitions. Cinema itself, due to its apparatus, proves a convincing means in which to represent the dyspastoral, the camera lens gazing at an inanimate landscape as an unresponsive 'sublime object'.[10]

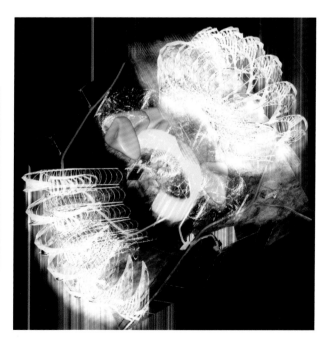

e Aling, Prounstretcher MMVIII, After *Better Things*, 2012
d in the Cotswolds of Duane Hopkins's *Better Things* (2008), couples' retreat invites each individual of a partnership to visit equence. Strained relationships are assessed while occupying ing real and unreal (virtual and cinematic) versions of the ounding landscape as a one-sided 'sublime object'.

Mike Aling, Prounstretcher MMI, After *This Filthy Earth*, 2012
An augmented-reality (non-religious) wedding venue in remote Cumbria. Augmented reality can potentially alleviate the increasing costs of wedding ceremonies and civil partnerships in the UK. In this scheme, urbanites can wash in a digitally wet augmented architecture that takes its precedent from director Andrew Kotting's *This Filthy Earth* (2001) – a manically grotesque, Bruegel-the-Elder-like cinematic interpretation of Émile Zola's novel *La Terre* (1887).

Proun Stretching

It would be misinforming to paint the Digital Cottage Industries project in an entirely gloomy light, given the repeated emphasis on the dyspastoral. The condition described above offers and encourages opportunities to re-colonise the urban ambitions of city exiles – to build industry and culture that floats across the landscape actually and virtually, a landscape that is beautifully elegiac. The dyspastoral as a theme has polemical potential, a means of questioning the political status quo of the (Western) city and opening up opportunities to envision socially democratic architectural systems in rural settings, with advanced technologies enabling such systems. In an age of globalised networks, Digital Cottage Industries posits small-scale architectures in order to resuscitate a sense of community akin to how traditional cottage industries functioned principally through (digital) industry, geographical proximity and human contact.

A couples' retreat, a credit union, an open-source software pavilion, a mobile library, a parcel distribution centre, a digital tool supplier, a home for an online educator and a wedding venue. The project develops a number of small-scale cyber-industry architectures that entwine actual with virtual spaces, sited into the landscapes of Britain's dyspastoral cinema (largely the production of British independent filmmakers with the exception of the occasional international auteur – Alberto Cavalcanti, Sam Peckinpah). The architectures are soft and palpitating, tuned to virtual urban rhythms that break free of urban planning restrictions mapped onto the countryside. The architectures hope to engage with issues of public space and social concerns in a largely privately owned and solitary actual rural territory, yet an increasingly complex digital meta city.

Digital Cottage Industries consists of a number of digital works, each an isometric model constructed to form a four-dimensional moving isometric image. Isometry itself is used as a representational tactic to draw equivalences between each site, architecture and digital city/country hybridity. The project takes direct formal inspiration from El Lissitzky's *Proun* series of geometric paintings produced between 1920 and 1925, updating, stretching and smearing their original potentialities. *Proun* explored an endless, expansive space free of gravity, presented in parallel projection with infinite points of entry and viewing positions. El Lissitzky enigmatically described this work as 'a place between painting and architecture, where painting changes trains'.[11] The Digital Cottage Industries work is cognisant of media theorist Lev Manovich's proclamation that digital cinema, the medium that the project is constructed for, is akin to a type of digital painting,[12] therefore siting the project between architecture and digital painting (digital film-making). Ultimately, the intention is that the works represent ubiquity, in opposition to the perspectival scopic regime that cannot help but compartmentalise our vision of the world. Digital Cottage Industries offers up a vision of the smeared, endless connectivity of our meta city, and of its socio-political and spatial potential in rural locations. ⏃

Notes
1. See article 'Cottage Industries Blooming Again' at http://news.bbc.co.uk/1/hi/northern_ireland/5350616.stm.
2. See www.theafricahouse.com/uniqueco-designs-kenya.
3. See article 'Ipad Spurs Cottage Industry of Digital Book Scanning Japan' at www.cultofmac.com/80486/ipad-spurs-cottage-industry-of-digital-book-scanning-japan/.
4. William Gibson, 'Life in the Meta City': www.scientificamerican.com/article.cfm?id=life-in-a-meta-city.
5. Jacob Emery, 'Art of the Industrial Trace', *New Left Review*, No 71, Sept/Oct 2011, p 121.
6. Fredric Jameson, 'The Politics of Utopia', *New Left Review*, No 25, Jan/Feb 2004, p 50.
7. This phrase is borrowed from film critic Gareth Evans. See Gareth Evans, '(Not) Gone to Ground', *Vertigo*, Vol 2, No 2, Spring 2002: www.closeupfilmcentre.com/vertigo_magazine/volume-2-issue-2-spring-2002/not-gone-to-ground.
8. Peter Hutchings, 'Uncanny Landscapes in British Film and Television', *Visual Culture in Britain*, Vol 5, No 2, 2004, p 29.
9. Beginning with *Went The Day Well?* (Director: Alberto Cavalcanti, 1942), set in an idyllic British village whose occupants form a classless cohesion after a covert Nazi invasion, and including *The Gamekeeper* (Director: Ken Loach, 1980), which is set in a rural enclave of private property and explores issues of an isolated lower middle class, the struggle of social mobility in rural climes and precarious employment on a seasonal basis.
10. 'Epistemologically speaking, cinema moves us by setting up a tension between that which gives and that which receives the gaze. People return looks in cinema, and if they evade them, that is meaningful … But the inanimate landscape can never interact … [Landscape] is the sublime object, since it raises consciousness while being itself immovable.' Sue Harper, 'The Ownership of Woods and Water: Landscapes in British Cinema 1930–1960', in Graeme Harper and Jonathan Rayner (eds), *Cinema and Landscape*, Intellect (Bristol), 2010, p 150.
11. See Eva Forgacs, 'Definitive Space: The Many Utopias of El Lissitzky's Proun Room', in Nancy Perloff and Brian Reed, *Situating El Lissitzky: Vitebsk, Berlin, Moscow*, Getty (Los Angeles, CA), 2003, p 50.
12. Lev Manovich, 'What is Digital Cinema? – Cinema, The Art of the Index', 1995, p 6: http://manovich.net/articles/.

In an age of globalised networks, Digital Cottage Industries posits small-scale architectures in order to resuscitate a sense of community akin to how traditional cottage industries functioned, principally through (digital) industry, geographical proximity and human contact.

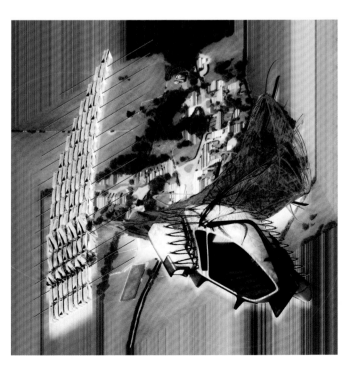

iPastoral

Architectural theorist and educator **Mark Morris** parallels the 18th-century enthusiasm for the Claude glass, a black mirror that framed and filtered views into painterly landscapes, with the current infatuation for a similarly small shiny black device with a capacity for taking picturesque images.

It must have seemed odd even to the 18th- or 19th-century tourist, who might be travelling – sometimes for days – to a beautiful natural site, only then to turn their back on the sought-after vista and view it in a small, slightly convex, black mirror. What were they thinking? These mirrors were all the rage and were used to capture picturesque scenes from nature by condensing and darkening the real thing, turning landscapes into instant landscape paintings in the manner of Claude Lorrain (1600–82). The Claude glass was a favourite of artists and aesthetes, soon becoming a must-have travel accessory.

The mirrors were handheld, usually oblong or rectangular with rounded edges made out of obsidian, tinted glass or glass backed with paint, jet or foil. They were heavy for their size and their shiny surface required they be carried in specially made cases, usually of leather, that could be flipped open like a book and kept in a pocket or travelling bag. Some were bigger and could be set up on an easel for artists intending to copy the contained scene onto canvas.

The longer one looks into a Claude glass – and real ones are notoriously hard to find outside of a few museum collections – the more one sees another world emerge. Even to eyes accustomed to Photoshop software and high-definition television, there is something compelling, even magical, about the way the convexity pulls a large view into a small frame, and how the black pushes the contrast and colour range into what one associates with the painterly. It seems a window onto another world rather than a mere reflection. What is more, it does not require Lake Windermere to be effective. Indeed, one of the joys of the Claude glass is using it to render anyplace outdoors, even one's own humble back garden, into a refined and evocative image.

The practice of using the Claude glass to view landscapes was not without its critics. Arnaud Maillet in his expert book on the subject (2004) reviews some of William Gilpin's (1724–1804) castigations ranging from, 'In general, I am apt to believe, that the merit of this kind of modified vision consists chiefly in its novelty' to 'the mirror is unable to present objects "with that depth, that gradation, the rotundity of distance, if I may so speak, which nature exhibits".'[1] Maillet himself acknowledges the artificiality represented by the Claude glass, but in artifice also identifies its merit:

Indeed, nature reflected in the black convex mirror is always fictive and incomplete, that is, lacking in relation to nature itself, because reflected (mechanical aspect) and reduced (fragmentary aspect) by this mirror. However, the double imperfection of nature's reflection tended to be supplanted, that is, idealized, by the mirror itself, for the reduction of the reflection removes numerous details and other particularities: the mirror tends to abstract.[2]

And it is this power of abstraction that persists in making the Claude glass more than a novelty. Part of its charm is had in how it abstracts with so little imagined effort. It is just a slab of slightly deformed shiny black material, yet it seems to do the work of a photographer savvy with special effects and filters. The repression of details, or rather the highlights that signal details, is central to the mirror's unique rendition. It is doubtful that Claude ever used black mirrors himself, but no one is in doubt that the mirror's reflection uniquely recollected his work, and his habitual subject matter – the pastoral landscape – is the other aspect, alongside the mechanical and fragmentary, that makes up the identity of 'his' mirror.

Born in Lorraine (his real surname was Gellée), Claude was active from about 1627 to 1682 and is credited with bringing Northern European landscape painting to Italy where it had been resisted as too secular. The elevation of landscape as a genre equal to the painting of mythic or religious scenes was in large measure instigated by his work. The poet Thomas Gray (1716–71), the mirror's famous proponent advocating its use to appreciate nature, links it squarely to the pastoral subject:

Claude Lorrain, *Landscape with Jacob Wrestling with the Angel, or Night*, oil on canvas, 1672
opposite: A forerunner of the landscape genre, Lorrain's work was stunningly new and daring in concentrating on landscape rather than narratives. Many of his paintings have a noticeably dark cast.

Claude Lorrain, Optical drawing aid, black glass in leather, *c* 1750–70
The resemblance to the iPad is uncanny. Depending on your subject, a rectangular or circular mirror could be deployed. Oblongs were also available.

I got to the Parsonage a little before Sunset, & saw in my glass a picture, that if I could transmit to you, & fix it in all the softness of its living colours, would fairly sell for a thousand pounds. This is the sweetest scene I can yet discover in point of pastoral beauty.[3]

While Claude's paintings have been persistently popular – John Constable (1776–1837) would sing his praises a century and a half later, describing him as 'the most perfect landscape painter the world ever saw'[4] – the Claude glass itself went out of fashion relatively quickly. John Ruskin (1819–1900) was not a fan, describing it as 'one of the most pestilent inventions for falsifying Nature and degrading art which was ever put into an artist's hands'.[5] The mirror got knocked generally for pulling people out of reality and into illusion, and specifically for functioning as a kind of cheat for artists who should be recording nature without the mediation of a gadget.

Yet there is a resurgent interest in what appear to be Claude glasses everywhere you look. People are glued to looking at small shiny rectangular black slabs with rounded corners, staring at them amidst the most demanding reality. When in the presence of natural beauty these latter-day Claude glasses are brought out reflexively to record the moment, fulfilling Gray's wish to transmit the scene. Transmission of data is the iPhone's purpose. That it looks so much like a Claude glass is accidental, but the resemblance – including the bigger mirror's likeness to an iPad – is uncanny. The way people tend to handle these devices, allowing them to take precedence over physically present people or places, or using them as status symbols, also weds them to the Claude glass. The habit of putting both in similar book-like cases is an indication of their shared fragility and worth.

The way to make an iPhone function like a Claude glass, of course, is to switch it off. No app[6] is needed to convert the high-tech mobile phone into a black mirror. The concavity is missing, granted, so there is no shrink-wrapping of the world, but the reflectivity on a black surface, the subtle tonality it presents, works just as well as the 'original'. The Claude glass was intended as an artist's tool, a means to frame and abstract reality in preparation for its representation on canvas. An iPhone's camera can be put to similar uses. Further, iPhone and iPad applications like 'Brushes' turn the devices into small digital canvases. David Hockney's recent flower still life and landscape work takes full advantage of this aspect. Few would use the darkened mobile itself as a mirror in aid of art, but contemporary artists are inspired by the object of the iPhone and recollections of the Claude glass.

Michael Tompert, designer-in-chief of the digital imaging and CGI firm Raygun Studio in Palo Alto, California, embarked on a series of images, collectively referred to as *12LVE*, showing the destruction of iPhones, iPads and the like. He states that this work 'provides society a *mirror*, forcing us to question our infatuation with mere objects'.[7] Tompert works digitally with photographs to produce impossibly detailed large-scale images. *Targeting* (2010) shows a 3GS iPhone shot through with a 9-millimetre

Heckler and Koch handgun. The spider's-web fracturing of the iPhone's screen refracts light as it dips towards the bullet hole's crater. A halo of oil – the iPhone's inky blood – emerges from behind. *Book Burning* features a 2010 iPad accosted by a soldering torch. The blackness of its screen is carbon melting away to reveal the circuit board.

Recent installation sculptures by Lauren Fensterstock explicitly recall the Claude glass. Working with paper and charcoal, she builds shallow reliefs that purge all colour save the dull reflection of curved or angled black paper. These are placed in black frames and sealed under glass so, from head on, they appear as dark reflections. Oblique views dispel this illusion, but offer up an unexpected depth. *Parterre* (2008) treats the same themes, but as room-sized pieces on the floor. Paper vegetation and rocks are set on pools of shiny Plexiglas backed with black, reflecting back the sculpture, the ceiling of the gallery space and its visitors peering down. The overall visual effect of the limpid pools and the delicate representation of nature upon them puts patrons in a pastoral scene, something Ruskin would have approved of.[8]

Michael Tompert, *12LVE [4] Targeting*, 2010
Tompert finds intricate beauty in the precise destruction of an iPhone. The facets of the bullet's crater catch the light in a range of iridescent colours.

Michael Tompert, *12LVE [4] Book Burning,* **2010**
Several layers of an iPad are revealed with its burning.
That the digital keyboard display persists under carbon
and fractured glass seems improbable.

Websites like Flickr and Instagram are seeing the emergence of online galleries devoted to amateur and professional photographers using iPhone cameras as well as application filters and effects to capture specifically pastoral scenes.

Lauren Fensterstock, *Black Mirror*, paper and charcoal under glass, 2011
top: Fensterstock's quadriptych repeats the proportion of a typical Claude glass. The floral studies she captures would not have been out of place in the late 18th century.

Erin Thurlow, *Untitled (iPhone)*, 2011
bottom: A high-tech eye patch or poor man's cyborg, Thurlow's arresting photograph captures the compulsive way many keep their eyes on their smart phones.

Erin Thurlow merges both iPhone and mediated vision in his project for his artist's residency in Chicago. His self-portrait (2011) features an iPhone taped over one eye. Packing tape obscures the screen and deforms Thurlow's face at the same time. His nose and ear are flattened and his mouth puckers, while his free eye still peers through a layer of the tape. The senses are warped by the device, and it has replaced half his ability to see.

Weakening our capacity to see was Ruskin's concern when it came to the Claude glass, much as he was interested in qualities of reflection and framing. For him, abstraction was good mental exercise, a way to build artistic ability and appreciation for the natural. It is a question of proximity to experience; if a painting is once removed from nature, painting with a Claude glass is twice removed. Tompert's photography/scanology permits excessive vision, showcasing details not normally picked up by the human eye. His images work in the opposite stance of the Claude glass in terms of abstraction. Conversely, Fensterstock's work is more abstract than a Claude glass image by virtue of being monochromatic.

Somewhere between these extreme conditions lives the Claude glass image circa 1800, the scene the tourists were after; picturesque in composition and pastoral in theme. The helpmate in seeing that vision, however sullied by critics of the day, the Claude glass continues to fascinate and invite scholarly research not least because, in form and function, it is recollected by the millions of iPhones in use today. Websites like Flickr and Instagram are seeing the emergence of online galleries devoted to amateur and professional photographers using iPhone cameras as well as application filters and effects to capture specifically pastoral scenes. An influx of picturesque images aping pastoral traditions and devices is now flooding social media. The genre as well as its associated gadgetry is back. ◬

Notes
1. Arnaud Maillet, *The Claude Glass: Use and Meaning of the Black Mirror in Western Art*, trans Jeff Fort, Zone Books (New York), 2004, pp 154–6.
2. Ibid, p 157.
3. See Joseph Wood Krutch (ed), *The Selected Letters of Thomas Gray*, Farrar, Straus and Young (New York), 1952, pp 152–3.
4. RB Beckett (ed), *John Constable's Discourses*, Suffolk Records Society (Ipswich), 1970, pp 52–3.
5. John Ruskin, *The Elements of Drawing in Three Letters to Beginners*, John Wiley and Sons (New York), 1876, p 210.
6. There is, in fact, a 'Reflection' application for Apple products, but it is used to turn a Mac computer desktop screen into something identical to the iPhone or iPad screens.
7. Michael Tompert, *12LVE, Artist Profile*, 1 June 2012. See www.tompert.com/12LVE/about/artist-profile.
8. See ET Coo and A Wedderburn (eds), *The Works of John Ruskin* (Library Edition), Vol 1, London, 1903, p 90.

ft: Detail of Lauren Fensterstock's *arterre*. The matte surface of the black per contrasts neatly with the sheen the watery Plexiglas. There is a nod traditional still-life composition and, rhaps, Ophelia.

Lauren Fensterstock, *Parterre*, paper, charcoal and Plexiglas, 2008
right: Fensterstock's large-scale installation lets patrons visually drift into the artwork. The scene conjures a funereal *Water Lilies* or scene from the film adaptation of *The Wizard of Oz*.

EXIST

STENCIL

Jeffrey James

Architect and interior designer **Jeffrey James** admits an ambivalent attitude towards nature. Here he turns that ambivalence to positive effect through a series of poetic digital collages that provide a mediation between 'our incomprehension of the vast magnificence and complexity of the natural world and the actual spaces that we can physically touch and inhabit'.

Ay, now am I in Arden: the more fool I. When I was at home I was in a better place; but travelers must be content.
— Touchstone, in William Shakespeare, *As You Like It*, Act II, Scene IV

It's All Too Big

I think we should invent or encourage a new status within the profession of architecture, that of the poet/architect. Whose job it is to go further than the Vitruvian ideals of firmness, commodity and delight, further than an artist whose engagement with nature we experience vicariously, but toward an architecture that mediates between our incomprehension of the vast magnificence and complexity of the natural world and the actual spaces that we can physically touch and inhabit. A natural poetic architecture that creates spaces that take us back into ourselves. Like attics, confessionals, the bed, the cloister or the study carrel. Small-scale containments validating, encouraging and prompting internal journeys. Spaces that are empowered by the vastness of nature and made habitable by the imagination offer a counterpoint to our increasing isolation from nature, from others and from our surroundings. This should be an architecture to help us connect more deeply with our inner selves and, consequently, more meaningfully engage with our environment and hopefully with each other.

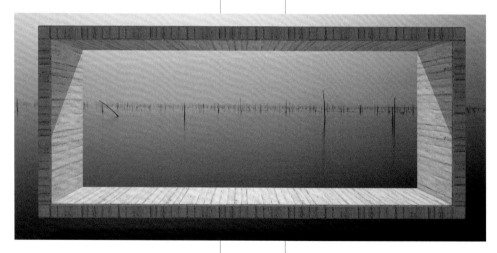

s All Too Frightening

ave been happily driving alone around Europe for a
umber of years, and during these contemplative journeys
began to notice that the passing landscapes were starting
unlock forgotten memories. Momentarily influencing my
oughts and feelings along the way: memories of childhood
ay in suburban parks, fragments of half-forgotten poetry,
rics of songs and half-remembered seminal texts would
urface into consciousness. My imagination would wander
and out of the car. Warm, secure and framed against
e cold, open and uninhabited. The moving against the
atic. An assuring touchstone between architecture and the
magination. I chose the technique of collage as a way to
ediate playfully between these states. The very medium
lping me to explore an ambivalence I have to nature. I was
rprised to find that the emerging architectural vocabulary I
bconsciously chose was dominated by a syntax of frames,
ntainments, bound or bondaged moments.

  Ossuary for the Invisible City (2008) was born from
series of experiences in Venice. Driving across the
a Libertà causeway that separates Venice from the
eneto, I saw the marine landscape in the early morning.
onversations with a Venetian friend came to mind, speaking
assionately about the scandalous quantities of toxic and
ghly carcinogenic chemicals emptied out into the lagoon,
nd about how Venice had lost its original purpose as a
ading city, now a hollow backdrop for tourists. I thought of
alo Calvino. The image of the calm lagoon littered with an
pparently arbitrary maze of course markers, channels for
goon traffic that no longer exists. The scene was one of
eath. Both beautiful and haunting. I was compelled to frame
like that of a Victorian memento mori.

Jeffrey James, *Basalt ablution room*, **digital collage, 2010**
top: A domestic shower room that treats washing as a ritual.

Jeffrey James, *A hole in Boscombe Pier*, **digital collage, 2008**
bottom: I dug a hole in the sand to bring my eyes level with the horizon. I was 8 years old at the time.

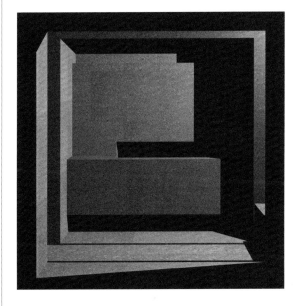

We're Just Too Small

In the 18th century, Immanuel Kant recognised that when faced with the magnitude of natural landscape we can only experience it as a sublime moment. By which he meant a feeling of awe mixed with terror. Werner Herzog, when making *Fitzcarraldo* (1982), commented on the jungle:

> It's not so much erotic, but full of obscenity. Nature here is vile and base. I see fornication and asphyxiation and choking, fighting for survival and growing and just rotting away … It's not that I hate it. I love it. I love it very much. But I love it against my better judgment.[1]

Resonating with my kind of ambivalence towards nature, they describe urban man's ongoing struggle to get closer to a nature that is far too big for our rational comprehension. To be physically exposed is to be vulnerable. In *As You Like It* (1599), William Shakespeare gets us, as urban dwellers, to imagine what life might be like living in a forest. Once again we are asked to decide: Is nature paradise or terror?

Shadow Line (2005) started from a dream in which I wrestled with an inexplicable urge to launch myself into the ocean despite an ominous sea mist rolling into shore and quiet voices offering warnings of danger. Nature experienced as a sublime moment, but with a route back to a safe vantage point that is a bench on a jetty. A space where one could find a place for oneself, both physically and psychologically, within the immensity of nature.

The architectural narrative of retreat emerged from the syntax and vocabulary. A language of enclosure that could exist within an inspiring yet frightening space. Like Alice's Wonderland, a utopian world. I began to explore notions of scale and accessibility. If 'small is beautiful', what size is 'small' in terms of a habitable retreat space in nature?

Opening the Fold (After Samuel Palmer) (2009) shows a landscape of apparent beauty, but the towering oaks underscore the contrast between the enduring laws of nature and the temporary laws of industrialised farming. Yet it remains inaccessible.

Scale and accessibility are firstly issues of psychology rather than of building. According to Theodore Roszak:

> Now the problem with that is that it has left us with a severely under-dimensioned psychology, a psychology in which the human mind does not connect with the natural environment.[2]

Roszak goes on to say that Sigmund Freud proposed that this idea of an under-dimensioned psychology was due to the horrors of the id:

> the aggressive and sexual instincts that we must protect ourselves from, might be thought of as a restatement of the theological notion of original sin that separated us from nature.[3]

Jeffrey James, *Opening the Fold (After Samuel Palmer)*, digital collage, 2009
top: Adrian Mole aged 16 once took a bus to the countryside. But it was closed.

Jeffrey James, *Wannsee Library*, digital collage, 2012
bottom: The empty library shelves are a testament to the books that were never written due to the decisions that were made in the house next to the woodland where the library is located.

Separated from Nature

Our current vision of nature in relation to buildings is distorted. In recent years, nature has come to be used in a highly representational way. Surface adornments of unwilling plants and shrubs cling on to expensively maintained, highly rationalised surfaces. Sad, dusty trees hanging on for dear life in dry office atriums.

In general, architecture is more than ever driven by global economics and evolving technologies. We live in an age that puts great emphasis on getting things done, and the machine is an efficient way of achieving this. By mastering technology, measuring, classifying, and exploiting the resources of the world, we think that we will solve all of our environmental problems. Even faced with empirical evidence that the earth's environment is turning on man's ability to live healthily on the planet, there are still many who doubt that there is a problem. Perhaps due to what Freud called 'collusive madness' or 'communal neurosis'. Most of us in the Western world cannot see it directly for ourselves and seem to have lost the instinct to comprehend it. As individuals, our psychological vantage point is either too small or there is an imbalance between the rational and intuitive sides of our brains.

But in art we can re-address the balance. As the character Alvy Singer in the Woody Allen film *Annie Hall* (1977) declared: 'You're always trying to get things to come out perfect in art because it's real difficult in life.'[4]

et the Music Begin

structure in the landscape, like a frame or a concrete
coustic mirror, can help to mediate between ourselves and
ature simply by standing in between. Creating a very personal
sonance. Like a magic key that unlocks our memories,
minding us that we are part of it all and not separate from
ture.

In constructing *Wannsee Library* (2012), I was unable
escape a deep irony. I came to see the calm, wooded
ndscape surrounding the villa where the Wannsee Conference
as held in 1942[5] through the voice of Sonia in Anton
nekhov's play *Uncle Vanya* (1897) describing the good Dr
strov's powerful and romantic view of trees: 'Forests are the
naments of the earth, they teach mankind to understand
eauty and attune his mind to lofty sentiments.'[6]

The First Note

And if a building is a frozen poem, then the materials used to
construct it are the carefully chosen words. Wabi-Sabi is the
ancient Japanese philosophy of aesthetics directed towards
the appreciation of objects, materials and things. It offers us a
way of appreciating the unquantifiable, the un-measurable and
the irrational. But mostly it gives us a poetic way of looking at
nature in beautiful contrast with its massive entropic forces.

> Materials vulnerable to the effects of weathering …
> forms of attrition are a testament to histories of use and
> misuse. Though things wabi-sabi may be on the point of
> dematerialization they posses an undiminished poise and
> strength of character.[7]

In *Study carrel for a London church* (2012), I have made
a retreat space that incorporates the corrosive effects of
weathering on bronze, not in lieu of nature, but nature itself
embodying its vast complexity. The surface as vast and
textured as a mountain range wrapping a table where a person
can sit and think. A retreat from the frenetic street life of an
urban centre.

The work strives to create an intimate moment of
engagement where there is a little reciprocity between person
and planet. Revealing the possibility of nature's great bounty
within a space that is in direct reach of all our senses. Like a
poem.

Architecture should be less concerned with rationalities
than it is with taking part in the process of coming-to-being and
revealing. To adopt the poet's vision into our view of the world.
To believe, like Goethe, that the essence of poetry is the same
as the essence of nature itself. ᴆ

Notes
1. Werner Herzog in *Burden of Dreams*, a documentary on the chaotic
production of making *Fitzcarraldo*, Flower Films, 1982.
2. Theodore Roszak in an interview with Jeffrey Mishlove for the television
series 'Thinking Allowed: Conversations on the Leading Edge of Knowledge
and Discovery with Dr Jeffrey Mishlove', Thinking Allowed Productions,
1998. See: www.williamjames.com/transcripts/roszak.htm.
3. Ibid.
4. Woody Allen, *Annie Hall*, Rollins-Joffe Productions, 1977.
5. The Wannsee Conference, held in January 1942, was where the Final
Solution was presented to the administrative leaders of the Nazi Party.
6. Anton Chekhov, *Uncle Vanya*, 1897, Act I.
7. Leonard Koren, *Wabi-Sabi for Artists, Designers, Poets & Philosophers*,
Stone Bridge Press (Berkeley, CA), 1994, p 62.

Jeffrey James, *Entrance to a
London church*, digital collage,
2012
top: A member of the
congregation said that before she
entered a room she would say a
little silent prayer: 'Let Christ go
before you.'

Jeffrey James, *Study carrel
for a London church*, digital
collage, 2012
bottom: Imagine if we all had an
intimate space as vast as that of
Saint Jerome's study carrel by
Jan van Eyck (Jan van Eyck, *Saint
Jerome in His Study*, 1442).

Alastair Parvin

OPEN

THE NEXT RURA

OPEN

FIELDS

DESIGN REVOLUTION

FIELDS

Alastair Parvin, an architectural and strategic designer at 00:/, calls for a focus on 'the opposite side of the urbanisation story: the impact that urbanisation has on rural areas'. He advocates a rural design revolution that re-engages with farming and the countryside as a site of intense production, rather than as a preserve for nostalgia and leisure activities.

Alastair Parvin, Server, Watford Gap, Northamptonshire, 20
The Server superstructure for biodiesel-producing microalgae not only avoids the problem of loss of land for food production, but actually intensifies use, integrating cattle farms, with leftover algal biomass as an organic feedstock.

You could be forgiven if, over recent years, you have lost count of the number of times an architect or a city mayor has begun a talk by citing that now, for the first time in history, over 50 per cent of the world's population live in cities. There is nothing wrong with this observation. It is important; the global population is urbanising, fast.[1] The problem is that having made the point, it is very often followed up with a weird, unexplained leap in logic. Usually the inference is that somehow, because of urbanisation, 'we must have more need of architects'.

When we stop and think about it, the implied proposition is that design, and in particular architecture, is really only concerned with 'the city': the spatial and social problems of density, mass, bigness, form. Architecture – narrowly defined as 'making buildings' – only seems to be concerned with one side of the coin. It treats cities as socio-geographic objects surrounded by a protected blank page; a green and pleasant land beyond the satanic mills. Architects do not belong there.

This simplistic dichotomy of 'city' versus 'country' is by no means exclusive to architecture: it goes deep into our popular culture, it is hardwired into our psyche, and encapsulated in our national governance and planning policies – illustrated brilliantly in Danny Boyle's Olympic opening ceremony. Since 1932, successive governments have perpetuated this conception of rural Britain not as a site of resource production, but as a cosmetic rural idyll and a wildlife habitat to be stewarded and preserved, but not turned to growth. By 2010, UK farmers produced only 52 per cent of the nation's food.[2] Rural Britain is now more a tourist attraction than a breadbasket.

Shared knowledge and open data will themselves be seen as renewable resources, fundamental to constructing a better urban-rural citizenship.

The Shrinking Rural Machine

By focusing so exclusively on urban conditions, designers are ignoring two inalienable realities.

The first is the opposite side of the urbanisation story: the impact that urbanisation has on rural areas. Rural regions with shrinking populations face an impossible dilemma, as conventional growth-based finance becomes inoperable.[3] Even in European social democracies, where the foreign outsourcing of production is compensated by agricultural subsidies or *appellations contrôlées*, demand from the super-wealthy for secor homes is creating massive rural social inequalities. One example of this was the Cornish fishing village of Helford, where the 2009 clash between production and preservation was played out as a planning dispute between fishermen and second-home owners. To one group, a jetty was a basic piece of industrial infrastructure, to the other it was an eyesore.[4]

The second reality is that, in truth, cities are not three-dimensional objects. What we see as 'the city' is, of course, a stage set, a grand illusion of stasis sustained by vast backstage machinery. Cities are the product of continuous production and supply of surplus: food, water, goods, energy, data. Industrialise nature. As Carolyn Steel articulates so lucidly in her book *Hungry City*,[5] the maintenance of this illusion depends entirely on the infrastructures that supply these goods: farms, distributic centres, motorways, pipelines.

It has never been easier to take these systems for granted. If we are hungry, we just go to Tesco. Yet, paradoxically, this also means we have never been so fully exposed to their failure. The rise of just-in-time logistics and the emergence of the food giants have created a food supply that is outwardly efficient, bu inwardly incredibly oil intensive. Richard Heinberg estimates that every calorie we eat requires 10 calories of fossil fuels to produce and deliver it.[6] In short, hardly efficient. Neither is the system resilient. It is an oft-quoted adage used by the security services that our cities only actually contain three days' worth o food – we are only 'nine meals from anarchy'.[7]

This means that issues of food security, climate change, water scarcity and the rising prices of food and oil present deep threats to the viability of cities themselves. The global trend towards urbanisation may seem unstoppable, but a chain of sudden, disruptive events in the supply system could see it local reversed, almost overnight.

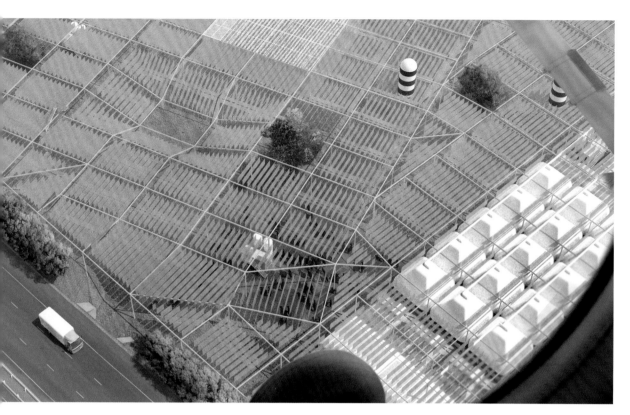

e Myth of 'Green' Architecture

chitecture does not yet have a language, or an economy, with ich to engage with this reality. When we confine design the city, to built form, we relegate it to a role where it can ly really deal with the fantasy of Arcadia – importing that tasy into cities in small, largely cosmetic doses. With the challenge of climate change laid out before it, architecture ers to technological add-ons and aesthetic reassurances: solar nels, green walls, glulam beams, hemp carpet. 'Buy more eco-hitecture.'

What 'green' design reveals is the extent to which we ntify very powerfully with the mythology of pastoralism ile neglecting the fact of it. We see endless proliferations the same aesthetic impulses: 'urban agriculture' applied like ologetic wallpaper to buildings; Barbour jackets in Chelsea; d turbines on supermarkets; or platitudes of support for ocal', 'organic', canvas-bagged consumer movement that convinced that all can be solved if only the poor could be rsuaded to shop at Marks & Spencer.

Against that, we are offered another choice, pitched as a re authentic environmentalism. It rejects the idea of progress, d advocates some sort of 'retreat to nature'. It demands with ignation that we must all change our behaviour and stop ing things that are, to most of us, inherently delightful: meat, idays, pets, red wine, chocolate.

As benign as this design ethic may seem, it rarely engages h the reality of the solution. In reality, there is no such thing nature that does not include us. The cow is a man-made cies. While retreating to the land may sound like an emotive l, and may be personally therapeutic, it is not practical or ially responsible. There is no 'better past' to be yearned Society itself (and the forms of progress it affords, such healthcare, education and human rights) is founded on the cialisation of labour and the production of surplus.

The problem with austerity environmentalism is that it offers an impossible set of political choices. It forces us to decide which forms of progress, wellbeing and delight we see as disposable luxuries, and whose. As a result, it inspires resistance and so-called scepticism. But above all, it denies the basic mathematics of population growth. It indulges in the idea of a simpler, more 'organic' life, unwilling to accept the true social and human cost of a retreat to food production solutions that are, as yet, lower yield and higher cost.

top: Strategic plan for a self-sufficient motorway. Here, a strip of the M1 in the Midlands is designated as a special planning zone, creating viable economic conditions for an entirely integrated artificial ecology.

bottom: Excess heat from agricultural processes creates moments of delight – leisure not bought but 'found' as an industrial surplus.

**Alastair Parvin and Lukas Barry,
Groundswell, Sipson, Hillingdon,
West London, 2010**
Each supporter funds a single
earthbag which, filled with earth from
near the site, collectively aggregate
to form a massive structure.

The Rural Design Revolution

By honestly facing up to the scale of the challenge, we can be
more optimistic about it. In the next few decades, we need to s
designers and architects engage in farming – in the reinvention
of the rural landscape as a site of resilient, sustainable, scalable
production, as well as a natural and cultural asset. This is an
incredible challenge: to re-imagine a radically new contract
between the city and the ecology that serves it.

As a proposition alone, this may seem a little abstract, unti
we begin to see the projects that emerge. The three projects he
can be used – not as last answers, but as first questions.

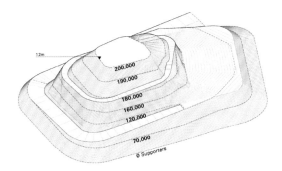

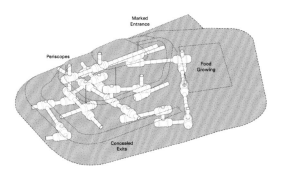

In the next few decades, we need to see designers and architects
engage in farming – in the reinvention of the rural landscape as
a site of resilient, sustainable, scalable production, as well as a
natural and cultural asset.

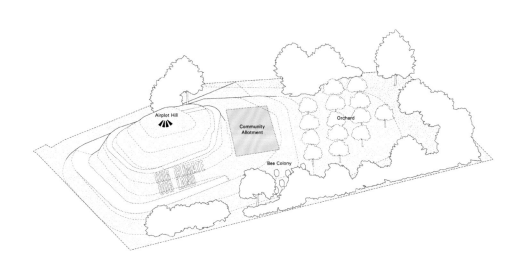

centre and above: Not a static product, but a carefully engineered process – of distributed design,
procurement and construction. No one individual can entirely know the final structure; a distributed,
'soft' strength.

bottom: Designed for Greenpeace UK in the path of the proposed third runway at Heathrow, the project
presents an unusual challenge: instead of having one client with thousands of pounds, it has thousands
of clients with one pound each.

rver: The New Infrastructure

ith the rise of China's economy, the West is just beginning to liscover the importance of infrastructure investment. Perhaps most visible part of this rural revolution will be a series of nning experiments, rethinking our oil-intensive network.[8] rver was one such proposition, taking a stretch of Britain's M1 otorway and researching the feasibility of its transformation o a self-sufficient farming belt: a closed loop of industrial, ricultural and cultural processes yielding fuel, meat, energy, ps and even data servers, without consuming fossil fuels or ducing any waste or pollution. It was not a pipe dream. It k data on existing processes, tools and capacities, and simply culated on their combined potential. What we could do if we ided to.

What emerged from the Server project were not just hnological solutions, but new cultural norms, strange l beautiful side effects that begin to break down the false tinctions between production, cultural identity and delight t late Modernism created. Much like the not-dissimilar ISA Offshore Membrane Enclosure for Growing Algae MEGA) project[9] (which was actually developed), the lessons are twofold. One, that economic viability forces egration – and that integration is more of a design challenge n innovation. Nothing can do just one thing. Second, that blic knowledge itself is one of the renewable resources in ecology. Suddenly, it becomes logical to imagine open-air imming pools heated by the excess heat from server farms, m houses at Watford Gap, carbon-positive logistics, local l on sale at petrol stations, and educational augmented reality the car. New infrastructure allows us to alter the habits of ached consumerism and build a richer (and, in fact, more ractive) idea of citizenship.

Groundswell: The New Economics

In 2010, Greenpeace and the local residents of Sipson village in West London bought a plot of land in the path of Heathrow Airport's proposed third runway, and allowed a community of 10,000 people (including the leaders of the two main opposition parties) to co-own it. An international competition was launched to design a physical and symbolic structure to fortify the site. The winning project, Groundswell, was, perversely perhaps, deliberately detached from the cause itself; it was an 'anti-monument'. Where a monument is a structure intended to impose the will of the few upon the many, this would be the opposite: a structure only as large as its popularity. Groundswell would not be a building as such, but rather an intricately designed procurement process, whereby each supporter would buy an earth-bag, onto which would be written their name. Aggregated and assembled according to a specific set of instructions, the result would be a man-made hill and orchard, the contours of which were a measure of people power; a literal 'groundswell' of support. If ever deployed, it will be the first structure in the world to be directly crowd funded in this way.

The subtext is that design can never be divorced from its economics. The engine of new rural development will be the mass-micro and sharing economy, amplified by the Web. The rise of cooperatives, crowd funding and peer-to-peer finance have huge potential to change the economics and politics of rural development.

Architecture 00:/, WikiHouse (global) open-source construction set
The aim of WikiHouse is to make it possible for anyone to adapt and use designs which they can assemble without power tools or traditional construction skills.

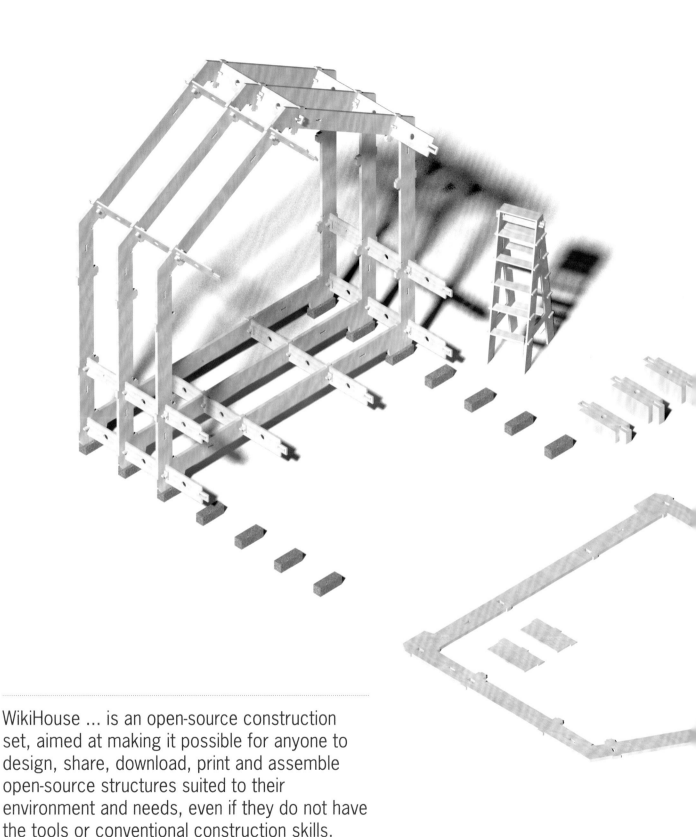

WikiHouse ... is an open-source construction set, aimed at making it possible for anyone to design, share, download, print and assemble open-source structures suited to their environment and needs, even if they do not have the tools or conventional construction skills.

Notes

1. United Nations, Department of Economic and Social Affairs, *Population Division: World Urbanization Prospects*, New York, 2012: http://esa.un.org/unup/.
2. DEFRA, *Overseas Trade Statistics*, 2012: www.defra.gov.uk/statistics/foodfarm/food/overseastrade/.
3. Rural Japan might be considered a possible bellwether. See Peter Matanle, 'Shrinking Sado: Education, Employment and the Decline of Japan's Rural Regions', in Philip Oswalt (ed), *Shrinking Cities: Complete Works 3 – Japan*, Project Office Philip Oswalt (Berlin), 2008, pp 42–53.
4. Jasper Gerard, Helford Divided by Fishermen's Dispute', *The Daily Telegraph*, 2 April 2009: www.telegraph.co.uk/earth/countryside/5093847/Helford-divided-by-fishermens-dispute.html.
5. Carolyn Steel, *Hungry City: How Food Shapes Our Lives*, Random House (London), 2009: www.hungrycitybook.co.uk.
6. Richard Heinberg, *The Oil Depletion Protocol: A Plan to Avert Oil Wars, Terrorism and Economic Collapse*, New Society Publishers (Gabriola Island, BC), 2006: http://richardheinberg.com/odp/getinformed/oilandfood.
7. Phrase originally coined by Baron Cameron of Billington reporting to UK government. Andrew Simms, *Nine Meals from Anarchy*, New Economics Foundation (London), 2008: www.neweconomics.org/publications/nine-meals-anarchy. *The Daily Mail*, 2008: http://www.dailymail.co.uk/news/article-1024833/Nine-meals-anarchy–Britain-facing-real-food-crisis.html
8. See, for example, Thanet Earth in Kent, a vast greenhouse, producing fruit and salad vegetables throughout the year: www.thanetearth.com/.
9. Jonathan Trent, 'Energy From Floating Algae Ponds, TEDTalk, June 2012: www.ted.com/talks/jonathan_trent_energy_from_floating_algae_ponds.html.
10. The Acts of Inclosure were British Acts of Parliament passed during the 18th and 19th centuries disbanding common land and placing it under private ownership.
11. The Open Source Ecology project is one early example of this, sharing designs for 50 open-source farming tools: http://opensourceecology.org/.

WikiHouse: The New Commons

Where the Acts of Inclosure[10] once commodified Britain's rural common lands, we are now seeing the emergence of a new commons – in knowledge and tools: for example, Wikipedia, the Linux operating system, software such as FreeCAD, and hardware such as the RepRap 3-D printer. The open-source design movement has radical implications for agriculture that we have barely yet seen: start-up farms experimenting with open-source tooling; robotics which allow permaculture techniques to be scaled up to something near industrial scale;[11] even open-source biotechnology. WikiHouse, being developed by 00:/ architects with an open community of collaborators, is one such experiment. It is an open-source construction set, aimed at making it possible for anyone to design, share, download, print and assemble open-source structures suited to their environment and needs, even if they do not have the tools or conventional construction skills. All the designs, the software and knowledge, are shared under a Creative Commons licence – by, and for, everyone. These commons – potentially serving not just our need for housing and shelter, but also for machinery, tools and off-grid infrastructure – could be thought of as 21st-century vernaculars, simultaneously global and local.

We may be on the brink of crisis – but design is also on the brink of huge opportunity. It is time now for architecture to look beyond the obsolete dichotomy between urban and rural; beyond 'building'. It is time to pay attention to the whole system, and to recognise that the integrative design thinking at which architecture excels might be at least twice as useful to society as we ever dreamt it might be. ∆

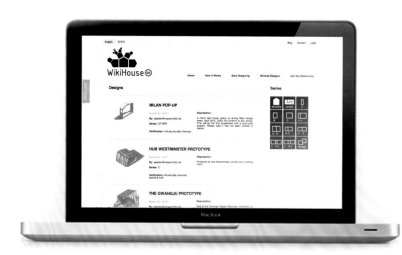

's can download and adapt house designs shared under a ative Commons licence, and using an open-source CNC machine, t' out the parts for the house from a standard sheet material as plywood.

NEXT-DOOR INSTRUCTIONS

For **François Roche**, the pastoral can threaten a phony eco-friendly dualism: 'It seems that our times have invited the two demons to the same cosy dinner party, thus provoking a divorce between the next door and the door after that – a permanent schizophrenia.' His research project, An Architecture 'des humeurs', thus seeks 'to confront the unknown in a contradictory manner'.

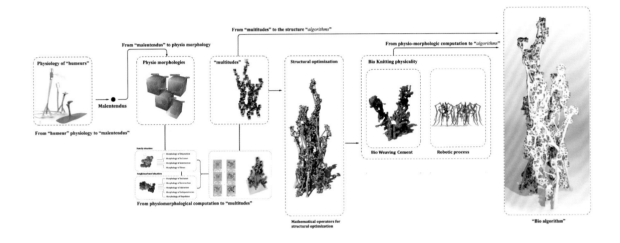

When pastoralism is trapped by Chaosmosis,[1] this increases the schizoid negotiation of double belonging and double membership, simultaneously framed by local instructions on 'living together' and, at the same time, a furious need to escape, to anywhere, similar to Dan Simmons's 'Transdoor',[2] opening a double window between the 'here, but ...' and the 'but elsewhere', to escape from the stuttering of the local forces of permanencies and immobility seeking to conserve a supposed 'authenticity' – that is, the existing situation – regulated by rules and policies ... to stop time ... a kind of revived Puritanism driven by society-friendly standards for 'good behaviour' and phony eco-friendly attitudes, moralistic totalising scrutiny, recipes for organic health food and over-moisturised soap for a perfect body in the ideal village, like the Truman Show, and in escaping all that, to fulfil irreducible needs like reaching, touching the forbidden, jumping through the only windows that authorise objectionable behaviour in the multiple infra-zones of the doors in electronic machinery (socialising, virtualising, fictionalising, pornoising, criminalising, and gaming the game) ... the legitimate need to HOPEFULLY be somebody else, the recognition of a contradictory, Siamese dualism, a symmetrical antagonism between the physical hoax of sedentary statements and the illusion of dematerialised nomadism, a permanent schizoid contingency, naturally intertwined.

It seems that our times have invited the two demons to the same cosy dinner party, thus provoking a divorce between the next door and the door after that – a permanent schizophrenia.

But this basic and symptomatic opposition imposes itself like a cliché, or more than a cliché – a new standard for 'life', or a caricature of life in which on the one hand there is the petrification of the local, and on the other side the artificialised eroticism of the illusory but necessary objective of freedom, like some natural compensation for the stone-edged statement of the former.[3]

For example, we could easily spend time in the 'bricolage-DIY-village-mall' to buy the perpetuation of what is already existing, to maintain the sclerosis of the environment by adding two limited screws and nails. We could easily buy a condo in downtown Chicago-Bangkok-Shanghai to simulate the happiness of 1950s urbanism transposed into a 'Peyton Place' or 'Pleasantville' vertical village, including swimming pools, the sports centre, the health-food shop and the security cameras, self-adapting to your shape for the ultimate comfort in sleeping equipment, with trendy 'flagshit' design selected by the latest issue of *Wallpaper*, including the latest ice-cube crushing fridge for your imported 20-year-old island Scotch, like the settings in Bret Easton Ellis's novel *American Psycho*,[4] but eviscerated of any psycho-human dimension, and in both cases meant to compensate for the degree of repressed emotion

New Territories/R&Sie(n), An
Architecture 'des humeurs', 2010–
Opposite: Step-by-step research:
psycho-morpho analyses, protocols of
aggregation, structural optimisation,
psycho-chemistry extrusion and robotics.

Bio-interview station. The physiological test sets a
baseline by measuring mind and bodily (de-)equilibrium
during a 15-minute interview as a bio-scan. It works
as an emotions sensor, collecting the biochemical
reactions (mainly molecules such as dopamine,
adrenaline, serotonin and hydrocortisone) that indicate

the atavism reaction of the subject (degree of pleasure
or repulsion, attraction or absence of interest) to
approach the cartography of unformulated desire, re-
questioning the gap, the malentendu between two types
of language, bio-psychism and free will. During the test
a kind of vapour (nanoparticles) is released.

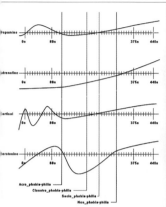

and sensation by providing a kind of discharging catharsis in the other window, operating in the depths of the network infra-zone, in the intimacy of the keyboard, the endless possibilities of personal and collective neurosis-psychosis that renegotiate human pathologies, the multiple identities syndrome, the temptation of insurrection through 'inappropriate language and attitudes' no longer tolerated in the physical planetary petit-bourgeois village.

This predictable, Manichaean yo-yoing between 'the next door and another door beyond' poses as the opposite of post-puritanical capitalism by simultaneously marketing the local and the global. This Siamese business plan traps our free will in a new double mass production of products and desires, from moralistic values about 'living together' to scatological, eschatological, compulsive and pathological gimmicks meant to serve as compensation, a transfer of missing parts.

In opposition, or just on the side, could we run an experiment in which the 'village' is a matrix across multiple doors, articulating the conflict immanent in living together without denying the uncertain, unpredictable nature of this conflict, directly revealing the sophistication or the lack of social contract, of neighbourhood protocols, to be adjusted in real time, articulating phantasm and reality, ugliness and beauty, obstacles and possibilities, garbage and fresh blooms, threats and various forms of protection, technicist prowess and forces

of nature, interlocked, in keeping with the vitality of the species inhabiting them?

Could we test some experimentation where 'architecture' is used as a strategy to subjectivise the real, the daily jingle, to negotiate simultaneously the contingencies of these dual-dimension needs of sedentary and nomadism, of security and risk, of certitudes and adaptations, as the antidote of the 'model owner', flattery that caresses human atavism, the weakness where we are most fragile, the ostentatious sycophancy of bogus social status that lies at the heart of the obscenity of the new 'world condo village'?

An Architecture 'des humeurs'

An Architecture 'des humeurs', a research project initiated in 2010 by New Territories/R&Sie(n),[5] seeks to create a kind of alphabet book of apparatuses, of knowledge strategies, to protocolise a counterproposal. It cannot be developed without re-evaluating all the tools, strategies, processes and the very raison d'être of technologies. As it navigates, it drifts from the psycho-methodology of collecting desires to the mathematics that interpret them as relationships, set-belonging situations, from psycho-chemistry to the logic of aggregation, from the physio-morphological computation of the multitude to C++ operators for structural optimisation as an artefact of a logic of discovery, from bio-knit physicality for the operation of a *below and bottom*: Physio + aggregative morphologies. Mathematical tools to translate the initial *malentendus* (contradictory desires) of belonging with set theory tools (inclusion, intersection, difference, etc) to extract a cartography of the mind (attraction, exclusion, touching, repulsion, indifference, etc) as a negotiation of 'distances' between the human beings (from themselves to their near environment).

Each initial habitable volume is composed of a 12-metre (39-foot) cube. The colonisation of this void is resolved by negotiation on distance between clusters (family members)/distance to distribution (lift-escape)/distance to the limits (facades)/distance to neighbourhood, interlacing the relationship between phobia/philia from the *malentendus* report.

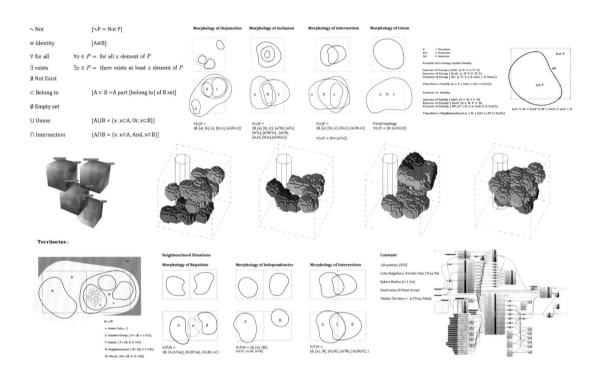

nonlinear geometry to a robotic process and behaviour, and from biochemical research to robotic design and G-code algorithms for automated manufacture.

Being political today is not a lazy fascination with slums, a social-political whitewashing such as was seen at the last Venice Biennale, in perfect symmetry with the mainstream, or the ridiculous PS1 programme over the last two years, trying to manipulate neighbourhood interest with a ping-pong table and a spiky Smurf to wash away the local pollution. It means defining a line of conflict, the aesthetics of conflict, a line of resistance and resilience,[6] a line of creation that infiltrates the cracks, the interstices between the chapel of power and the self-assurance of the powerful, questioning the order of discourse, human free will, the uses and abuses of mathematics, technological imperialism and necessity, machinist arrogance and the potential of narration to infiltrate and de-alienate the ghetto of expertise and control promoted by power – and, at the same time, contradictorily, to work for the emergence of a bottom-up strategy of knowledge by means of computational/DIY urbanism, neither mimicking favelas nor denying science, adopting neither positivism and its mysticism nor its opposite, a regressive nostalgia, but, through a mimesis of their evolutionary vitality with its (un)certain trajectories, human pathology, conflictual apparatuses and contingencies, seeking to achieve a sophisticated and unique assemblage of and for the people that architecture was originally supposed to 'dominate'.

below top: Structural optimisation strategies and procedures. Mathematical process to obtain incremental and recursive optimisation (exo-local, local and hyper-local) that simultaneously calculates and designs the structural elements supporting the physio-morphologies. The shapes are made only through successive iterations that join the morphologies by physically and structurally

coagulating the space between them, so that they can support each other both individually (local calculations) and as clusters (exo-local calculation). The calculation meets precise inputs (constraints and characteristics of the building material, initial state, dead load and transfer of forces, intensity and vectorisation of these forces).

below bottom: 3-D print of outputs from the previous calculation.

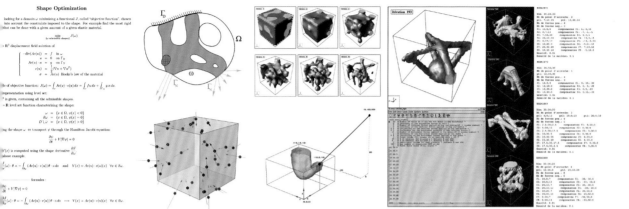

Top Down and Bottom Up

How can we reconsider the notion of space, a term used to death by modernity, of a 'living zone' understood not in terms of repetitive stereotypes or a modernistic promenade, but as a way to generate multiple singularities, a polyphony of multiplicity, a multitude, where architecture engages and generates empathy, sympathy and, naturally, antipathy as a factor in relationships, a transactional operator, a vector of negotiation between each of us and others to bring back together the 'elsewhere' and the 'here, and yet', the 'near and far', stability and nomadism, the 'village' as a secure sensation, a whispering *Heimat*,[7] and at the same time to hear the scream of its intrinsic forces of transformation as its vitality overflows.

Looking beyond a strictly scientific and architectural horizon, and reading beyond the usual philosophical benchmarks, it is tempting and, indeed, enlightening to envisage a modus operandi from a metaphorical and strategic angle in which exploring the 'chemistry of bodies' often envisaged as an element liable to disturb and alter linear, authoritarian logics, can achieve what we might call aggregations of 'swarm'[9] intelligence. Similarly, it is tempting to look at the relationship of the body to space, and even more, of bodies in their social relations: not just their interrelation within a given cell, but also their intra-relations as part of an osmosis with others. This results in an architecture that plays with conformism and conventions, and instead offers an 'undisciplined' conception of production in its articulation of the collective and the political.

An Architecture 'des humeurs' constitutes the second leg (after I've heard about, in 2005)[10] of an architectural voyage (in the spirit of Thomas More's *Utopia* of 1516) federating the skills of scientists from a host of disciplines (mathematics, physics, neurobiology, computations, scripts, nanotechnologies,[11] robotics). This exploration is an attempt to articulate the real and/or fictional link between geographical situations and the narrative structures capable of transforming them. Specifically, the focus here is on using nanotechnology to collect physiological data from all participants to prepare and model, by means of these 'moods' – a (post)modern translation of Hippocrates' four humours – the foundations of an architecture in permanent mutation, modelled (and modulated) by our unconscious. It is an investigation into an architecture of uncertainty and indetermination.

An Architecture 'des humeurs' is an interrogation of the confused region of the psyche that lies between pleasure/desire and need/want. It works by detecting physiological signals based on neurobiological secretions and thus achieving a 'chemistry of humours', treating future property buyers as inputs who generate a range of diverse, inhabitable morphologies and the relationships between them. The groundwork comes from a rereading of the *malentendus* inherent in the expression of human desire. Those that traverse public space through the ability to express a choice by means of language, on the surface of things, and those that are underlying and perhaps more disturbing but just as valid.

The possibility of structure as a logic of resistance, emerging a posteriori to become inhabitable morphologies, calls into question the traditional client–architect relationship and offers an alternative way of generating forms.

By means of the latter we can appraise the body as a desiring machine with its own chemistry: dopamine, hydrocortisone, melatonin, adrenaline and other molecules secreted by the body itself that are imperceptibly anterior to the consciousness these substances generate. Thus, the making of architecture is inflected by another reality, another complexity, breaking and entering into language's mechanism of dissimulation in order to physically construct its *malentendus*, including the data that the acephalous body collects that can tell us about its adaptation, its sympathy and empathy, in the face of specific situations and environments.

The collection of humours is organised on the basis of interviews with a hundred people that make visible the conflict and even schizophrenic qualities of desire, between those secreted (biochemical and neurobiological) and those expressed through the interface of languages, to make palpable and prehensible the emotional transaction of the 'animal body', the headless body, confronted with the mutation of a situation, the drifting of an environment. The protocol was to generate a reactive emphasis of phobia-philia inputs and to record, using the emitter-sensor-detector feature, the biochemical evolution of the 'mind' and read this data as relationship outputs comprising psycho-perturbation and psycho-stuttering as a result of attractor-repulsor emotional contingencies.

Mathematical concepts borrowed from set theory are used as a strategic relational tool to extract from these multiple 'misunderstandings', a morphological potential (attraction,

exclusion, touching, repulsion, indifference) as a negotiation of the 'distances' between humans and humans, humans and limits, humans and access that constitute these collective aggregates.

This branch of mathematics was founded by Georg Cantor in the late 19th century. Its aim is to define the concepts of sets and belonging (union, inclusion, intersection and disjunction). This theory can be used to describe the structure of each situation as a kind of collective defining the relationships between the parts and the whole, while taking into consideration that the latter is not reducible to the sum of its parts (or even the ensemble of relationship between the parts). It is becoming the matrix, the combinations for the relational structure on which an inhabitable space allows for the definition of all the properties of a given situation in relational modes, both the relationships between the elements themselves (residential areas) and those between these elements and the ensemble or ensembles. It describes morphologies characterised by their dimensions and position in the system and, above all, by the negotiations of distance they carry out with the other parts and as multiple artefacts, produces relational protocols, relational relationships and relational aesthetics: protocols of attraction, repulsion, contiguity, dependence, sharing, indifference, exclusion.

These relational modes are simultaneously elaborated within the residential cell and on its periphery in relation to

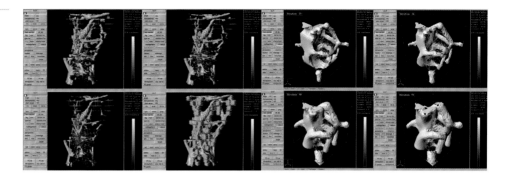

the neighbouring colonies. The multiplicity of possible physio-morphological layouts based on mathematical formulations offers a variety of habitable patterns in terms of the transfer of the self to the other, and to others as well. The data obtained from the physiological interview by means of nanoparticles concerns the following issues: familial socialisation (distance and relationship between residential areas within a single unit), neighbourhood socialisation (distance and relationship between residential units), modes of relations to externalities (biotope, light, air, environment), and also seeing, being seen and hiding, modes of relating to access (receiving and/or escaping, even self-exclusion) and the nature of the interstices (from closely spaced to panoptic).

In contrast to the standard-model formatting of habitats, this tool offers contingencies that produce the potential to negotiate with the ambiguities of one's own humours (tempers) and desires. It enables the mixing of contradictory compulsions (appearances) and even some *malentendus*: 'I'd like that but at the same time/maybe/not/and the opposite.' These *malentendus* are directly influenced by the pathologies generated by collective living, oscillating between phobia and philia (claustro-agora-xeno-acro-nocto-socio-neo phobia/philia).

The secondary goal of the research, in terms of mathematical development, concerned structural optimisation, defining the structural sustainability of the system as a post-production. The possibility of structure as a logic of

resistance,[12] emerging a posteriori to become inhabitable morphologies, calls into question the traditional client–architect relationship and offers an alternative way of generating forms. Emancipated from the conceptual logic where the structure is the starting point, the spatial contract takes the place of the social contract. Since it is conceived a posteriori, the structure is reactive, adaptive to multiplicity, as the permanent discovery of new agencies, entities and singularities.

Within the framework of this research, François Jouve developed a mathematical process for 'empirically' seeking optimisation, by creating forms out of constraints and not vice-versa.[13] The structural optimisation algorithm differs from directly calculated structural methods such as calculating the load-bearing structure of a building after it has been designed. In contrast, the algorithm allows the architectural form to emerge from the trajectories of the transmission of forces simultaneously with the calculation that generates them. The algorithm is based on (among other things) two mathematical strategies, one taken from the derivative initiated by the research of French mathematician Jacques Hadamard (to modify a shape by successive infinitesimal steps, to improve the criteria we want to optimise, as a permanent variation of boundaries) and the other from the protocol of the representation of complex shapes by Cartesian meshing through level set (to understand *below top*: Bio-cement weaving (material expertise). Development of a viscous and adherent secretable material so as to produce this morphologically complex structure. This is a bio-cement component, a mix of cement and bio-resin developed by the agricultural polymers industry that makes it possible to control the parameters of viscosity, liquidity and polymerisation, and thus produce chemical and physical agglutination at the time of secretion.

below bottom: Robotic process, behaviour and design. Developme of a secretion and weaving machine that can generate a vertical structure by means of extrusion and sintering (full-scale print) using a hybrid raw bio-plastic cement that chemically agglomerates to physically constitute the computational trajectories. This structural calligraphy works like a machinist stereotomy comprising success geometrics according to a strategy based on a repetitive protocol

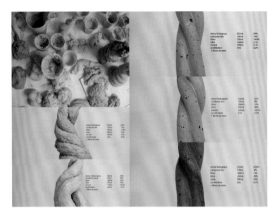

locally what could be the line of the highest or lowest resulting point, if we project the local incremental iterative calculus onto a 2-D diagram, to extract the X,Y position in the space as data to be re-injected into the next step of the calculation.)

This strategy of incremental and recursive optimisation (ex-local, local and hyper-local) approaches simultaneously calculates and designs their trajectories, supporting the multiplicity and heterogeneity of physio-morphologies. Following the non-deterministic aggregation of the unpredictable overstacking of desires, the structural branching and coagulation are generated by successive iterations of calculations that physically link the interstices between morphologies so that they can support each other locally and globally. The calculations satisfy precise inputs, including the constraints and characteristics of the materials used, initial conditions, dead load, and the transfer of forces, intensity, and vectorisation of these forces.

The third part of the research was to define a construction protocol able to handle complex, non-standard, non-repetitive geometries through a process of secretion, extrusion and agglutination. This frees the construction procedure from the usual frameworks that are incompatible with a geometry constituted by a series of anomalies and singularities.

The key is the development of a secretion and weaving machine that can generate a vertical structure by means of extrusion and sintering (full-size 3-D printing) using a

hybrid raw material (a bio-plastic cement) that chemically agglomerates to physically constitute the computational trajectories. This structural calligraphy works like a machinist stereotomy comprised of successive geometrics according to a strategy based on a non-repetitive protocol. This machine, both additive and formative, uses a bio-cement component, a mix of cement and bio-resin developed by the agricultural polymers industry that makes it possible to control the parameters of viscosity, liquidity and polymerisation, and thus produce chemical and physical agglutination at the time of secretion. The mechanical expertise of this material is made visible (by constraints of rupture induced by traction, compression and shearing, and so on).

The mathematical process of empirical optimisation makes it possible for the architectural design to react and adapt to previously established constraints, instead of the opposite.

Through the use of these computational, mathematical and mechanisation procedures, the urban structure engenders successive, improbable and uncertain aggregations that constantly rearticulate the relationship between the individual and the collective, between top down and bottom up, and that reactivate the potential for the self-organisation and creativity of the multitude in pursuit of the metabolism developed by Constant Nieuwenhuys and Guy Debord.[14]

Notes

1. The title of Félix Guattari's last book: *Chaosmosis: An Ethno-Aesthetic Paradigm*, Indiana University Press (Paris), 1995.
2. Transdoor is a kind of 'farcasting', a kind of 'Beam me up, Scotty' carried out in the domestic zone of a basic and banal apartment. Dan Simmons, *Hyperion*, Doubleday (New York), 1989.
3. Second Life description in the film *The Cat, the Reverend and the Slave*, by Alain Della Negra and Kaori Kinoshita, 2009.
4. Bret Easton Ellis, *American Psycho*, Vintage Books (New York), 1991.
5. '*Humeurs*' in French is not easily translatable into English, and this is why we kept it in French. It means 'mood', 'temper' and 'fluids' in the sense of Hippocrates' four humours: blood, yellow bile, black bile and phlegm. See: www.new-territories.com/blog/architecturedeshumeurs/. The research was carried out with mathematician François Jouve in charge of working out the dynamic structural strategies; with the architect and robotics designer Stephan Henrich;

Winston Hampel and Natanael Elfassy on the computational development, with the help of Marc Fornes; and Gaetan Robillard and Frédéric Mauclere on the physiological data-collection station, following a nano-technologies scenario by R&Sie(n)-Berdaguer & Pejus. The research has been funded by the Laboratoire-Paris: Director David Edwards, Curator Caroline Naphegyi.
6. The research is organised on several levels: from the physiology of humours to misunderstandings; *malentendus* (a word that can be translated as 'misunderstandings' or 'mishearings'); from the misunderstanding of humours to physio-morphological computation; from physio-morphological computation to the multitude; mathematical operators for structural optimisation; the 'algorithm(s)'; from the 'algorithm(s)' to bio-knit physicality; toolings/robotic process; and tooling/bio-cement weaving (material expertise).
7. '*Heimat*' is a German word that has no simple English translation, denoting the relationship of a human being towards a

certain spatial social unit. It is often expressed with terms such as 'home' or 'homeland'.
8. François Roche, *Reclaim Resi[lience] stance*, Log 25, Summer 2012.
9. In the sense of the word as used by Toni Negri and Michael Hardt in *Empire*, Harvard University Press (Cambridge, MA) 2000.
10. See Neil Leach, *AD Digital Cities*, July/August (no 4), 2009, pp 40–5.
11. Nano receptors can be inhaled, making it possible to 'sniff' the chemical state of the human body. Like pollens, they are concentrated in the bronchia and attach themselves to the blood vessels. This location makes it possible for them to detect traces of stress hormones (hydrocortisone) carried by the haemoglobin. As soon as they come into contact with this substance, the phospholipidic membrane of the nanoparticles dissolves and releases several molecules, including formaldehyde (H_2CO) in a gaseous state. The molecules rejected by the respiratory tract are detected using cavity ring-down spectroscopy (CRDS). This is a method of optical analysis using laser

beams programmed to a particular frequency, making it possible to measure the density of airborne molecules. The wavelength used for the detection of formaldehyde is around 350 nanometres.
12. 'A scientist, a mathematician, creates a function … it is mainly an act of resistance … against the wishes of casual opinion … against the whole domain of stupid questioning … Creation is resistance … it is the production of exaggerations … and their existence is the proof of their resistance … against stupidity and vulgarity.' Gilles Deleuze, *Abecedarium*, 1988–9, an 8-hour-long video interview about his philosophic ideas and concepts in alphabetical order: 'A' for Animal, 'B' for Boisson (drink), 'C' for Culture, 'D' for Désir (desire), 'E' for Enfance (infancy), 'R' for Résistance and so on.
13. Shape optimisation (C++ on Linux, developed by François Jouve).
14. In the Amsterdam Declaration, Amsterdam, 10 November 1958, reprinted in Internationale Situationniste #2, December 1958.

Through current technologies and procedures we can 'un-achieve' what we could call 'computed slums': we can re-question and refresh the democratic delegation of power between bottom-up swarm whispering and top-down tooling. Animist, vitalist and machinist, An Architecture 'des humeurs' rearticulates the need to confront the unknown in a contradictory manner by means and tools that are normally used to enhance control and prediction, expertise and anticipation. In contrast, it expects to give rise to multitudes in their palpitation and complexity, and the premises of a relational organisation protocol, where the village is a process in progress, a matrix that is not a final product but determined by outputs from the multitude of desires, of *malentendus*, recognising human pathology as a process of discovery. ⌂

all above: Nonlinear knitting extrusion. Development of a construction process that can deal with complex, non-standard geometries through an agenda of secretion, extrusion and agglutination.

Duncan Berntsen

PASTORAL MANOEUVRES

ECOLOGIES OF CITY, NATURE & PRACTICE

In the 21st century, the greening of public open spaces has proved one of the most compelling marketing teasers, but also one of the biggest 'elephants in the room'. Architect, educator and urban designer **Duncan Berntsen** describes how students within the School of Architecture, Design and Construction at the University of Greenwich were encouraged to tackle this by developing 'measurable innovative disruptions' that could contribute positively to an urban sense of place.

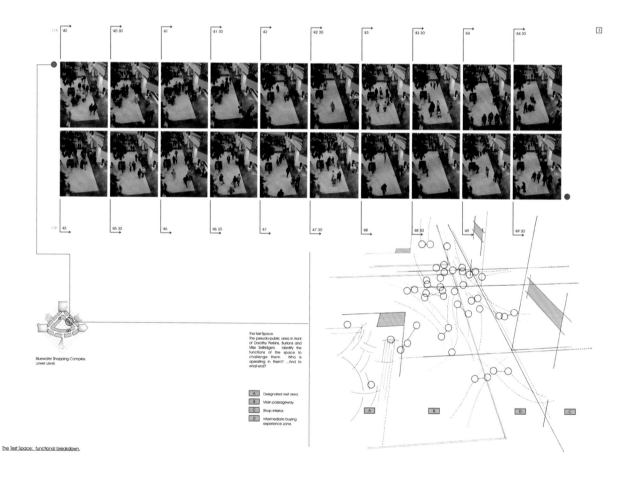

Lydia Schilbach, Bio-Acasa: Quad-Helix and Interaction Impacts, Barcelona, Spain, Diploma in Architecture, School of Architecture, Design and Construction, University of Greenwich, London, 2003
The Etzkowitz and Leydesdorff triple-helix approach to university–industry–government relations for innovation[1] was here extended, proposing culture and society as a fourth helix and bringing community to the heart of innovation processes.

ace is something built-environment
rofessionals seek to define and market
a renderings of oven-ready spaces for
evelopments that neglect the social and
ological ongoing returns that green
frastructures offer. While too often used
s an advertising sop, more profitable and
ngaging returns remain unseen due to their
tangible nature. The opportunities and profits
at planted open public spaces offer investors
e actually the 21st century's green 'elephant
the room'; it cannot be seen due to its
st and intangible nature and hence remains
articulated.

The 'pastoral' is in fact an intangible rather
an physical construct, and this intangible
ement has increasing value much needed
our cities and economies. Its heart lies
notions of simplicity, charm and serenity;
cadian contentment lying deep in the psyche
our populations. The idealised, imaginary
d hence intangible scenes of traditional
astoral culture were frequently used to foster
olitical belief, propaganda and action, but can
ese intangibles be defined and articulated
day to commodify public spaces, making
em more accessible and valuable, and hence
ailable contributions to the value chain?
y defining the obscure character of the
astoral as intangibles of the Arcadian idyll,
e can begin to communicate it, value it and
xchange it. Over the past decade staff and
udents within the School of Architecture,
esign and Construction at the University
Greenwich have sought to render a
tionale upon which investment decisions
extraordinary public infrastructure can
e confidently founded. From the not-so-
ivolous expense of an advanced-tech aviary
r a peacock flock, to the use of a humble
ectrical substation as a community incubator,
e projects have been seen as measurable
novative disruptions that contribute positively
the intangible value chain of places as
vestable and tradable proposals; 'generator
oducts' rather than 'end products' of
eighbourhood feedback and value.

The 'performance of the city' can be
considered as the sum output from a vast
number of interactions between its human
resources. In this context, a park or public
space should be considered to have a 'balance
sheet' contribution; the 'balance sheet of
place'. Using indicators and navigators,
correlations can be made between spatial
configuration, thematic and incidental use or
service provision and bottom-line performance
through which programmatic juxtapositions
of unexpected human interfaces and nature
can be valued. Seen collectively as intangible
ecologies able to be harvested for innovation
and value, they are not scale dependent to
render investable benefits. Hence a balcony, a
blade of algorithm-receptive grass, temporary
3G land forms or a strategically placed
apple tree can all offer investment returns,
collectively acting at multiple scales.

These ideas were explored by students
of the Diploma in Architecture and MA Urban
Design programmes at Greenwich. For
example, in Yi-Xing-Bo, a district of Tianjin city
in China, students and staff were invited to
uncover disruptive yet productive forces that
sustained the district and fed the city with
immigrants from the countryside. The district
acted as a halfway house in the broadest
sense between the urban and rural. The
looseness of the environment gave a portal
and support to country entrepreneurs wanting
to enter the city with their ideas, energy and
wares within ecologies akin to a natural urban
incubator.

Yi Xing Bo Urban Workshop, China, MA Urban
Design, School of Architecture, Design and
Construction, University of Greenwich, London,
2006
below top: Part landscape, part urban, scruffy, loose
and profitable, this edge city harboured an exuberant
concern for ongoing husbandry and was unexpectedly
influential regionally, yet appeared to be unmanaged.
Its place on the threshold of city and country led to a
rich layering of multiple functions and urban/country
exchanges.

below centre: A significant proportion of Tianjin's
fledgling entrepreneurial activity and small and
medium-sized enterprises started life in a pastoral
milieu within the city not unlike that shown here.
Country workers had relocated their sheds to the
edge of the city and in so doing had created the
foundations for a form of place infinitely more
inventive, engaging and relevant, from which they and
the rest of the city would profit and move on.

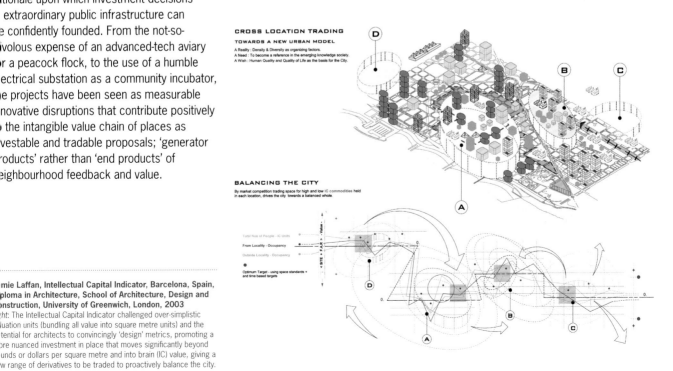

CROSS LOCATION TRADING
TOWARDS A NEW URBAN MODEL
A Reality : Density & Diversity as organizing factors.
A Need : To become a reference in the emerging knowledge society.
A Wish : Human Quality and Quality of Life as the basis for the City.

BALANCING THE CITY
By market competition trading space for high and low IC commodities held
in each location, drives the city towards a balanced whole.

mie Laffan, Intellectual Capital Indicator, Barcelona, Spain,
ploma in Architecture, School of Architecture, Design and
onstruction, University of Greenwich, London, 2003
ht: The Intellectual Capital Indicator challenged over-simplistic
luation units (bundling all value into square metre units) and the
tential for architects to convincingly 'design' metrics, promoting a
ore nuanced investment in place that moves significantly beyond
unds or dollars per square metre and into brain (IC) value, giving a
w range of derivatives to be traded to proactively balance the city.

The pastoral can offer an accessible rationale to demand a more nuanced spectrum of personable operation with neighbourhood care, responsibility, husbandry and knowhow at its heart. Pastoral holistic development invites us to invest in the benefits of a holistic multi-local, multilayered system.

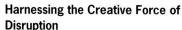

Harnessing the Creative Force of Disruption

Seeking to redesign the current valuation and investment system, the projects shown here served to collectively demonstrate that higher-order patterns of 'holistic' functions in the built environment cannot be predicted or understood by a simplistic summation of its parts or layers. Not surprisingly, unforeseen profits emerged as the components interacted in complex, unforeseen ways; something we know through everyday life but which is little recognised by the professions who more typically attempt to base valuation on square metres. These reductionist methods of valuing opportunities within the built environment undermine the true human costs and benefits of, or simply ascribe enhancements to, 'the market' as a whole. The pastoral can offer an accessible rationale to demand a more nuanced spectrum of personable operation with neighbourhood care, responsibility, husbandry and knowhow at its heart. Pastoral holistic development invites us to invest in the benefits of a holistic multi-local, multilayered system.

Developments in industry and business have generally taught us the importance of the continuous improvement at the heart of conventional industrial processes, education, architecture and research. It is holism, however, that favours creativity and adaptability. But it is what kind that is an issue for municipalities that try to differentiate themselves. GDH, a 'happiness index', as a corollary to GDP, has recently become currency among the G8 countries, who have recognised that the creativity for their success within knowledge economies will be rendered by self-actualisation; the highest order within Maslow's hierarchy of needs[2] – broadly, happiness. Cities and municipalities competing for global 'talent attraction' to support their competitiveness may have an unexpected bedfellow in the Arcadian contentment of the pastoral. Configuring the spatial and governance conditions for the disruptive force of creativity, adaptability and innovation to have the freedom for productive life is increasingly becoming a priority for municipalities within developed economies.

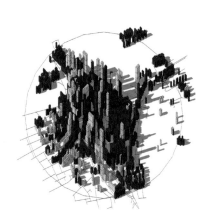

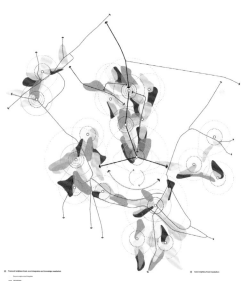

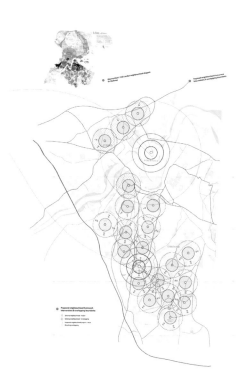

Andrew Dowding and Yogesh Patel, Medway, UK, MA Urban Design, School of Architecture, Design and Construction, University of Greenwich, London, 2008
Dowding and Patel's Medway projects developed tools and means of representation that moved from tech-enhanced analogue to fully digital early big-data methods to exploit more granular manipulation of the metrics for opportunity creation.

cologies of Everyday Practice

e ecology of the city, architecture and
e approach to green and public space
n, and needs to, be richly layered and
ghly original to satisfy the intangible
turns upon private investment being
ught today. This ecology of practice
well positioned within the nuanced
re and diverse scale of interests of
e pastoral, and has the legitimising
arion call of past ages to rally
ceptance of its bundled attributes.
needs a framework of research and
actice within which a growing body
evidence, tools, methods and value
n be developed, framed and tested.
pastoral, holistic architecture and
actice needs to be accountable and
dically creative to be effective beyond
mple energy saving. To be sustainable,
chitecture should now reclaim the
nfidence to design a great many more
pects of a place than the building
elf. ◬

Notes

1. A triple helix of overlapping yet relatively independent institutional spheres to capture contemporary innovation processes. The triple-helix model attempts to account for a synthesis between opposing principles in which new resolutions are found that allow several tasks to be accomplished, even as each influences the other. This has had much influence on contemporary innovation and economic development theory. L Leydesdorff and H Etzkowitz, Triple Helix issue of *Science and Public Policy*, Vol 25, No 6, December 1998.

2. Maslow's hierarchy of needs is a theory in psychology proposed by Abraham Maslow in his paper 'A Theory of Human Motivation', originally published in *Psychological Review*, 50, 1943, pp 370–96. These theories have been made much of in organisational management and development. His full theory was published in AH Maslow, *Motivation and Personality*, Harper (New York), 1954.

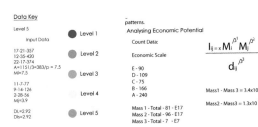

Data Key

Level 5

Input Data

17-21-357
12-35-420
22-17-374
A=1151/3=383/p = 7.5
Mi=7.5

11-7-77
9-14-126
2-28-56
Mj=3.9

DL=2.92
Dis=2.92

● Level 1
● Level 2
● Level 3
○ Level 4
● Level 5

patterns.
Analysing Economic Potential

Count Data:

Economic Scale

E - 90
D - 109
C - 75
B - 166
A - 240

Mass 1 - Total - 81 - E17
Mass 2 - Total - 96 - E17
Mass 3 - Total - 7 - E7

$$I_{ij} = x \frac{M_i^{\beta^1} M_j^{\beta^2}}{d_{ij}^{\beta^3}}$$

Mass1 - Mass 3 = 3.4x10^{46}

Mass2 - Mass3 = 1.3x10^{48}

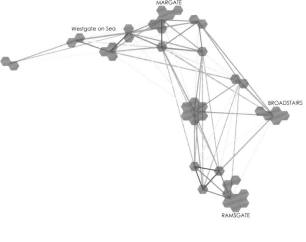

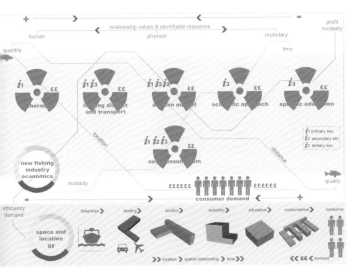

 yyam Sahni, R&D Fish Market, Great Yarmouth, Norfolk,
, Diploma in Architecture, School of Architecture, Design
d Construction, University of Greenwich, London, 2007
D Fish Market developed indicators that identified and measured
ationships, impacts, values and trends within the soft underbelly
the fishing industry in Great Yarmouth and rendered them visually
stakeholder negotiation.

Jake Basset, Integrated Indicators, Thanet and Staffordshire,
UK, MA Urban Design, School of Architecture, Design and
Construction, University of Greenwich, London, 2010
top and above: Integrated Indicators demonstrated how de-risking
development could be approached through spatially modelling
the interaction of agents and indicators upon each other within
the digital realm. This could be done by combining big data and
the experiential to manipulate risk mitigation and value creation
feedback loops towards a holistic ecology of influences.

COUNTERPOINT

Kevin Rhowbotham

ET IN ARCADIA EGO ET IN ARCADIA EST

Architect, academic and broadcaster **Kevin Rhowbotham** scrutinises the reasoning and value of the New Pastoralism project. He dispels the Arcadian impulse as 'a specious and mythicised image of the rural', calling upon architects to seek a true understanding of rural conditions in relation to the urban.

Thomas Cole, *The Course of Empire: The Arcadian or Pastoral State*, **oil on canvas, c 1836**
A reinvigorated late Renaissance determination of the Arcadian pastoral after Claude Lorrain; a timeless and ahistorical bucolic image of things incredible and never existent.

at confounds the popular imagination in this godless time
non-believing is the concept of nature; and it is the concept
nature in opposition to the concept of man which finds
e, if any, foundation upon which to build an ethics. Nature
the antithesis of man; it is the end of man and the ending of
humanity (when man is dead the universe will continue). In
ture, both the beginning and the ending of all things human
l be fashioned. Let me put this succinctly: nature and culture
e opposites, not merely opposed; they are antithetical. Nature
chaos until culture, by means of a will to fashion it, derives
ltivated and cultivating perspectives. Nature is not the real,
Plato would have it,[1] but rather it is precisely a 'nothingness'
ter Nietszche) or an ending *sub specie aeternitatis*, a
nouement perhaps; and, after Spinoza, God itself, *Deus
ve Natura*, precisely a totality.[2] Either way it stands behind
human will to construct it; to construct a life. Culture is not
erely order, an ordering of things, but the very landscape of
der, its geography, history, topography and stratigraphy; the
ry notion of conceivability is something altogether human.
e beautiful, the truth, the good, the real, the natural have no
nceivable existence beyond human life and can be attributed
aspects of the universe in the first instance only as a
nsequence of human aesthetical deliberation.

HE METAPHYSICS OF ESSENCE

Faustian 'will to control'; that aspect of consciousness
hich reflects the Enlightenment notion of progress within
e pervasive structure of a globalised, one might even say
odernist, ideology, seeks mastery as a prime objective over
e caprice of nature at the cost of spiritual independence
aust trades his soul for omniscient insight and becomes the
stroyer of worlds). Such a notion of control can and must
oceed only from a perspective that is exclusively human. It
not, and never can be, the imposition of yet the latest stage
the progressive development of human enlightenment and
derstanding, structured teleologically (with respect to an end
use) towards an absolute ethics.

A Platonic metaphysics assumes that the world is grounded
tra-perceptually; that it retains a substantial and irrefutable
sence behind the denotation and connotation of things. This
the old view and the timorous view of those who will not
cept the world as it is. Such a metaphysics of 'fixedness', a
etaphysics of essence' if you will, obtrudes both Christian and
atonic views of the natural, seeking to ground them finally and
rmanently within a general category.

Thomas Eakins, *Arcadia,* **oil on canvas,** *c* **1883**
An insistent dialectic of innocence and guilt consumes this
image, most certainly from our own perspective. The decay
of an immaculate pastoral vision is subsumed beneath the
apparently mythical figures, both sexual and innocent.

Perfidious Albion

The concept of the natural pervades the anti-urban
consciousness of ENGLAND, a name which itself rings with
the mythologising precepts of Arcadia, the bucolic and with a
palpable sense of a lost Golden Age. Not that ENGLAND as a
concept has a right to exist under the implied omniscience of
a singular and grounding ethics of the global and the 'all the
same' in which any 'rights of man' have been reduced to a series
of mannerly requirements in a despairing attempt to constrict
common opinion with a tourniquet of political correctness, for
gross political ends.

Little England …

This royal throne of kings, this sceptred isle,
This earth of majesty, this seat of Mars,
This other Eden, demi-paradise,
This fortress built by Nature for herself

… once rich with diversity and eccentricity, is straining
under the heft of a contrived global togetherness, crushing
heterogeneous temperament. Any reverie of the natural serves
only to compound the anomie of urban disaffection and never
to purge it. In ENGLAND all is rural, glimpsed as if from the
rear window of a deracinated and desiccated urban garret. In
ENGLAND the world is glanced at, disinterestedly, from the
back garden.

Identität Denken

Notions of the rural, struck from this alloy of mythical precepts, are a persistent foil for projections of identity. For architects, and for too long, this has been a predominantly urban identity. The rural remains an escape route along which so many crypto-urban caprices can be channelled. There is nothing remaining in contemporary architecture which is not always and already urban, and this as a consequence of the universal acceptance of a grounding and globalising Modernism.[4] The rural such as it remains in the architectural imagination takes on what Kenneth Frampton once called the 'communicative or instrumental sign'.[5] A sort of mythologised image, massaged by the technological spectacle,[6] which sublimates the desire for direct experience by obviating a critical praxis; (the image of the rural is the rural) … a popular response in which immanence, a direct and erotic experience,[7] immediate and visceral, is denied the viewer, yet simulated, fetish like, within and behind an image.

What Are Words Worth?

One might venture that architects, in so far as they remain thinkers at all, are suckers for identity, but then humans think habitually of identity, and architects are surely human; all too human. Some have argued (intellectuals not architects) that identity is the primary intellectual paradigm[8] by means of which the world is 'languaged' and given communicable form.

The meaning of intellectual objects such as 'urban' and 'rural' are forged in terms of ranked categories, subsumed under a general concept heading. The proper noun 'Architecture' is a case in point. *In rei veritate*[9] Architecture has no material existence as a name. It is a descriptive term that subsumes material instances. To speak of Architecture universally in this way is to speak of nothing at all; only examples of architecture exist, be they buildings, writings, readings, drawings or any other performative and reflective occurrence. Problematically, within an extended political discourse, the proper noun 'Architecture' is hypostasised,[10] giving itself up as a target for the extension of power interests through regulation and celebrity. Hence the Royal Institute of British Architects (RIBA), the Architects Registration Board (ARB) and other world regulating bodies commandeer the term, assuming regulatory power over it. In a like manner, celebrated architects and those who contrive celebrity and thereby authority within the discourse (magazines would be a prime example) attempt the same appropriation.

COMMODITY ARCHITECTURE

Ironically, at this moment in the wheel of history, the business of transforming qualities into quantities, and qualities into categories, is the tribal teleology of all that calls itself Architecture; as with much else under the aegis of neoliberal capitalism. Certainly architecture today is a game of categories in which a pious nominalism precedes critical thinking at every conceptual level. It is the formation of the general category and the control of the general category that establishes the grounding of commodity architectural

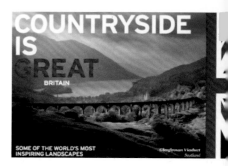

VisitBritain advertising campaign 'Countryside is GREAT Britain'
Frampton's communicative or instrumental sign. The affectation of the image presumes a shared and constant association between an idealised bucolic vision and the countryside, and the 'greatness' of Britain.

structures ('styles' as the magazines would like to have it) th. have altogether displaced any examination of the acute socio political issues that surround the discipline.

Terms such as 'parametrics', 'landscape', 'interactivity', 'morphogenesis', 'programming' and 'cyberspace' conflate random examples under general category headings, each vying for commodity advantage, each as incomplete and reified as the other. Self-evidently nothing material is at stake other than the eternal expansion of the architectural market; nothing is solved and nothing analysed, nothing is criticised determined substantially or with any prospect of social effec Social specificity and historical debt is never countenanced, no one is served, and no one is materially illuminated; only general categories are collected and extemporised *sub rosa,* for the purview of the 'elect'. But a private architecture is no architecture at all; an isolating agenda which regards architecture as an autopoiesis of self-referential concerns risks leaving life well out of the picture; and if there is no social product to architectural speculations of this kind, there is little social benefit.

The terms 'urban' and 'rural' are opposed as general categories and as grounding categories (as categories which support a metaphysics of essence); as targets against which the propensity of architects to seek out universals can be aimed. Consequently, when, as at this vertiginous moment in socio-political consciousness, the concept of the urban is conceived to be in crisis, drawn up against other empirical, not to say millennial narratives such as global warming, global cooling, the revenge of nature (El Niño), the retreat of polar ice, global food shortage, global economic depression the end of oil, systemic corporate corruption, the implosion of democracy, the death of God, need I go on … a ready substitute is assumed. When the current concept of 'city' ceases to support a general mythological need for grounding the concept of 'country' will satisfy.

HE COUNTRY AND THE CITY

erhaps the most influential text on the perception of the
ban/rural opposition was penned in the early 1970s by
aymond Williams. In his celebrated book *The Country and
e City*,[11] Williams argues that the vision of the rural retains
tirely a contemporary concept of the bucolic, lost to a fallen
ciety. The idea that a 'constant and continuous rural life', a
structure of timeless and un-shifting order, has been fatally
dermined by the city, Williams shows to be a permanent
pect of literary reflection and literary imagination, dating
ck at least to the 16th century. The 'dark mirror' of the
y is held up as the antithesis of the bucolic, projecting
downfall and disappearance, leaving the evils of the
sufferable city inescapable. In equal measure and in direct
ntradiction, early Modernist authors, most especially in
ance and Germany as opposed to the UK and the US,
fer an interpretation of the modern city as a haven in which
pects of modern life and contemporary mores can be
rsued anonymously, in the bosom of the teaming masses,
vay from the prying eyes of a morally constricting rural
mmunity.

The connotation of country and city as structural images
rvades the popular imagination as polarities between which
e ravages of successive crises of capitalism are hung.
nereas the rural countryside offers mythical reference to a
st Golden Age and a haven from the instrumental failures of
dustrial capitalism, the city harbours the Faustian apologue
enlightenment progress and all that it promises under
e magnified attention of a contemporary proselytising
formation culture. Both images are, according to Williams,
myth functioning as a memory'[12] that dissimulates class
nflict, enmity and animosity, ripe within both structures,
ost in evidence at times of structural crisis within capitalism.

e Image of the Rural

turn in desperation to a specious and mythicised image
the rural as a relieving alternative to the evils of the
ban, to find solace in a trivialised and disingenuous
yth of a 'green and pleasant land', to wistfully invoke the
nblematic memories of the English Romantic poets (Shelley
otwithstanding) as a bellwether of socio-political sentiment,
dream of a lost and forsaken Avalon persisting beneath
e detritus of urban capitalism, is to long for a return
something that never achieved any material existence
hatsoever.

What is required from architects is a critical understanding
an imminent agrarian reality in opposition to the globalising
ty, and a critical approach to regional relations. Such
modesty of work that seeks to understand the actual
onditions of the rural in relation to the urban, under the
rall of globalising tendencies, is conspicuously absent.
hat is certainly most unwelcome is yet another architectural
ommodity, structured under a generalising rubric such as
rchitecture and the Rural' , 'Rural-ism' or 'Rural Architecture',
oselytising yet another vacant and politically hollow formalism
at desperately struggles to leave some mark, any mark, on
e empty page of architectural thinking. ᴆ

Notes

1. Frankfurt School thinkers and in particular:

> Adorno unequivocally rejected the view that philosophy and
> the exercise of reason afforded access to a realm of pristine
> thoughts and reality. In stark contrast to those rationalists such
> as Plato, who posited the existence of an ultimate realm of
> reality and truth underlying the manifest world, Adorno argued
> that philosophical concepts actually expressed the social
> structures within which they were found.

See Andrew Fagan, 'Theodor Adorno (1903–1969)', Internet
Encyclopaedia of Philosophy, Section 3, 'Identity Thinking and
Instrumental Reason': www.iep.utm.edu/adorno/#H3.
2. The universe is a single substance, hence God and nature are the
same thing. See Baruch Spinoza, *The Ethics*, originally published in
Ghent in 1667 as *Ethica, ordine, geometrico, demonstrata*.
See Baruch Spinoza, *The Ethics and Selected Letters*, trans Samuel
Shirley, Hackett Publishing Co (Indianapolis, IN), 1982.
3. See William Shakespeare, *King Richard II*, Act II, Scene I.
4. See the opening paragraphs of Kenneth Frampton's post-Frankfurt
School account of the progressive globalisation of corporate
architecture in Kenneth Frampton, 'Towards a Critical Regionalism:
Six Points for an Architecture of Resistance', in Hal Foster (ed),
Postmodern Culture, Pluto Press (London), 1983, pp 16–30.
5. Ibid.
6. See Guy Debord, *Society of the Spectacle*, trans Fredy Perlman and
Jon Supak, Black and Red (Detroit, MI), 1970; revised edition 1977.
Online at: Library.nothingness.org.
7. See Susan Sontag's plea for the establishment of an Eroticos:
Against Interpretation and Other Essays, Delta (New York), 1967, pp
275–92. Orignally published in Partisan Review 4, 1964.
8. See Theodor W Adorno, 'On the Dialectics of Identity', in *Negative
Dialectics*, Continuum International Publishing Group (London), 1981,
pp 149–51.
9. Saying it like it is.
10. Hypostasise: to treat something abstract as a material thing; to
subsume a thing beneath an abstract category.
11. Raymond Williams, *The Country and the City*, Oxford University
Press (Oxford), 1975.
12. Ibid, p 47.

Norilsk, Russia
The irradiated endgame of Modernism. This is what the bucolic
fantasists fear they will inherit.

Mike Aling is Design Co-ordinator of the Diploma in Architecture programme at the University of Greenwich, where he co-runs Diploma Unit 15, a graduate design unit specialising in the use of film and animation to propose architectural concepts and interventions. His research interests include the utilisation of film and animation (theory and production) in architectural education and practice, open-source software communities, and the socio-political implications and opportunities afforded by the use of advanced technologies in architectural design.

Duncan Berntsen is a Fellow of the Royal Society of Arts, academician of the Academy of Urbanism, and a visiting professor at the Hebei Institute of Technology in China. He has been academic leader for MA Urban Design and PG Architecture at the University of Greenwich in London, is a mentor for the Creative Pioneer Program at NESTA (Inspiral), and is founder and first chair of the 1st East design panel in the UK. He has held directorships in some of the UK's largest plcs and is currently designing and consulting in private practice. His primary interest has been the development of innovation environments for public, private and academic stakeholders, having studied taught and practised architecture, urban design, spatial planning, property risk and value management, building conservation and business administration in the UK, US, Asia and West Indies over some 30 years.

Matthew Cannon and Mascia Gianvanni are ex-students of Mark Titman, and directors at FutureScape Studio, a practice based in London and Moscow. Current projects include the refurbishment of Vnukovo International Airport and high-profile residences in Moscow. Their international lifestyles allow for broader, universal thinking. They are interested in ecology, philosophical dialectics and nonsensical fun, and are currently debating the merits of living either in the city or countryside.

Nic Clear is a qualified architect, and currently Head of the Department of Architecture and Landscape Architecture at the University of Greenwich, where he also teaches a design

unit that specialises in the use of film and animation in the generation, development and representation of architectural spaces. He is particularly interested in the intersection between architecture and science fiction. He was guest-editor of the *Δ Architectures of the Near Future* (Sept/Oct 2009) issue, and has also written the 'Architecture' section of the forthcoming *Oxford Handbook of Science Fiction*.

Kathryn Findlay is widely regarded as one of the most outstanding architectural design innovators of her generation. With Ushida Findlay Architects (UFA) she has built ground-breaking projects in Japan, the UK and the Gulf. Her work is known for being responsive to different contexts: historic, contemporary and cultural, with an emphasis on being sensitive to circumstances and listening to the needs and tastes of the client. She prides herself on taking this from her Scottish countryside roots. UFA's architectural philosophy is the marriage of programme and poetry. The practice was at the forefront of pioneering free-form design, which was the principal reason for the firm being invited to work with Arup, Cecil Balmond and Anish Kapoor on the ArcelorMittal Orbit for the London 2012 Olympic Village.

Colin Harrison has worked in the Ashmolean Museum, Oxford, since 1991, and is now Senior Curator of European Art. He has a particular interest in landscape painting and in John Ruskin and his interpretation of the natural and man-made environment. He has arranged numerous exhibitions, on JMW Turner, Ruskin, the Pre-Raphaelites and others.

Jeffrey James was trained as an interior designer at Chelsea School of Art and Hornsey School of Art in London, and completed his architectural studies at the Royal College of Art (RCA) in 1985. He began his career with Marcel Breuer Associates in New York, followed by work with Ettore Sottsass and the Memphis Design Group in Milan. In 1987, he launched his own private architecture and interior design practice, specialising in design-and-build projects. He has also established a workshop for manufacturing architectural

specials, furniture and lighting. He has taught interior design at Richmond College, London, and is a frequent guest juror with the RCA, the Architectural Association (AA) and the Bartlett School of Architecture, University College London (UCL). He has been a visiting lecturer at the architectural school of Greenwich University for the past eight years.

May Leung is a young architect who has worked with Amanda Levete Architects in London on The Huntingdon Tower, and internationally in Hong Kong, on a commercial complex and on a residential tower in Dubai and, currently, in New York where she is working with developers to gain experience in applying her interests. Her interests in local social sustainability and the application of practical social landscapes are in contrast to the large commercial projects she has worked on. In the future she aims to design and build her own small-scale projects in ways that question our preconceptions of materials and ownership. She has spoken at 'The Green Forum' at Greenwich University, and at the RCA, where she graduated in 2009.

Gregory Marinic is Director and co-founder of d3. He is Director of Interior Architecture and Assistant Professor of Architecture at the Gerald D Hines College of Architecture of the University of Houston. He is also principal of Arquipelago, a New York- and Houston-based interdisciplinary practice in architecture, interiors and branding that has been awarded by the Seoul Metropolitan Government, AIA, IFRAA, Socio-Design Foundation and the ACSA, and published in the US and internationally. Prior to independent practice, he worked in the New York and London offices of Rafael Viñoly Architects. He serves as an associate director of *AIA Forward* journal, and editor of the *International Journal of the Arts in Society, Design Principles and Practices, IDEC::Exchange* and *d3:dialog*. He is currently pursuing a PhD in architecture at Texas A&M University where his research focuses on utopianism and diasporas.

ark Morris is an architectural theorist and ucator. His books, *Automatic Architecture: signs from the Fourth Dimension* (College Architecture, UNC-Charlotte, 2004) d *Models: Architecture and the Miniature* ohn Wiley & Sons, 2006) focus on ual representation and notions of scale. e studied architecture at the Ohio State niversity and completed his PhD at the ondon Consortium supported by the BA Research Trust. He teaches at Cornell niversity where he has served as Director of raduate Studies.

astair Parvin is an architectural and ategic designer at 00:/ architects in ondon. He is co-creator of the TED ize-winning project WikiHouse, and -editor of *Makeshift* (www.bemakeshift. uk), an open fanzine about architecture, onomics, technology and society. In 2010 s Groundswell project, designed with kas Barry, was selected as winner for the eenpeace 'Airplot' project at Heathrow.

arta Pozo Gil is an architect and licensed EED/BREEAM assessor. She has been orking since 2007 with MVRDV where, addition to her role as a project leader, e leads the practice's Sustainability epartment. By forming environmental ategies and energy-efficiency guidelines each design process, she ensures a high andard is maintained for all of MVRDV's ojects. She received degrees from niversidad Politécnica de Valencia (2001) d Technical University in Berlin (2004). e lectures regularly and has won several ards.

hn Puttick studied architecture at the niversity of Nottingham and the Bartlett hool of Architecture, UCL. His diploma oject entitled *Land of Scattered Seeds* s been exhibited internationally, and a py was purchased by the Museum of odern Art (MoMA) in New York for collection. Upon graduation he joined vid Chipperfield Architects, and has bsequently worked at Make Architects. nce 2008 he has lived in Beijing where he ds Make's work in China.

Kevin Rhowbotham is an award-winning international architect, academic and broadcaster. A Fulbright scholar, he graduated from Cornell University School of Architecture with subsequent doctoral studies at Cambridge University. He has held professorial posts in urban design and architecture at the Technical University in Berlin and at the University of Illinois at Chicago. Following the publication of his two ground-breaking books, the influential *Form to Programme* (Black Dog Publishing, 1995) and *Field Event/Field Space* (Black Dog, 2001), he achieved an international reputation as a theorist lecturing in 15 countries worldwide. He currently holds the Chair in Architecture at the University of Central Lancashire.

François Roche is the principal of New Territories/R&Sie(n)/[eIf/bʌt/c]. He is based mainly in Bangkok and New York, and sometimes in Paris. Through these different structures, his architectural works and protocols seek to articulate the real and/or fictional, the geographic situations and narrative structures that can transform them. His architectural designs and processes have been shown at, among other places, Columbia University, New York; UCLA, Los Angeles; the ICA in London; Mori Art Museum, Tokyo; Centre Pompidou and Musée d'Art Moderne in Paris; Tate Modern, London; and Orléans/ArchiLab. Works by New Territories/R&Sie(n) were selected for exhibition in the French Pavilion at the Venice Architecture Biennales of 1990, 1996, 2000 and 2002, and in the International Pavilion in 2000, 2004, 2008 and 2010. Among the teaching positions held by Roche over the last decade are guest professor at the Bartlett School of Architecture, UCL, in 2000, the Vienna TU in 2001, the Barcelona ESARQ in 2003–04, the Paris ESA in 2005, the University of Pennsylvania in Philadelphia in 2006, the Angewandte in Vienna in 2008, the USC-Los Angeles in 2009–11, and currently at RMIT in Melbourne and Columbia-GSAPP.

Dominic Shepherd currently resides in a wood in Dorset. He exhibits widely both nationally and internationally, and recent exhibitions include 'Black Mirror', with John Stark, at Ambacher Contemporary, Munich, and 'Jerusalem' at Charlie Smith London. He is also an associate lecturer at the Arts University Bournemouth. Both his practice and research are concerned are with notions of romanticism, folklore, the arcane and the poetic experience.

Michael Sorkin is Principal of the Michael Sorkin Studio, a global design practice working at all scales with a special interest in the city and green architecture. He is also President and founder of Terreform, a non-profit institute dedicated to research into the forms and practices of just and sustainable urbanism, President of the Institute for Urban Design, and Distinguished Professor of Architecture and Director of the Graduate Program in Urban Design at the City College of New York. He is the author or editor of more than 15 books on architecture and urbanism.

Geoff Ward received a BA in biology at Liverpool University before going on to study architecture. He is currently in private practice and has taught at a number of architecture schools in the UK.

Liam Young is an architect who operates in the spaces between design, fiction and futures. He is founder of the think-tank Tomorrow's Thoughts Today, a group whose work explores the possibilities of fantastic, perverse and imaginary urbanisms. He also runs the Unknown Fields Division, a nomadic workshop that travels on annual expeditions to the ends of the earth to investigate unreal and forgotten landscapes, alien terrains and industrial ecologies. His projects develop fictional speculations as critical instruments to survey the consequences of emerging environmental and technological futures.

INDIVIDUAL BACKLIST ISSUES OF △ ARE
AVAILABLE FOR PURCHASE AT £22.99 / US$45

TO ORDER AND SUBSCRIBE SEE BELOW

What is *Architectural Design*?

Founded in 1930, *Architectural Design* (△) is an influential and prestigious publication. It combines the currency and topicality of a newsstand journal with the rigour and production qualities of a book. With an almost unrivalled reputation worldwide, it is consistently at the forefront of cultural thought and design.

Each title of △ is edited by an invited guest-editor, who is an international expert in the field. Renowned for being at the leading edge of design and new technologies, △ also covers themes as diverse as architectural history, the environment, interior design, landscape architecture and urban design.

Provocative and inspirational, △ inspires theoretical, creative and technological advances. It questions the outcome of technical innovations as well as the far-reaching social, cultural and environmental challenges that present themselves today.

For further information on △, subscriptions and purchasing single issues see: www.architectural-design-magazine.com

How to Subscribe

With 6 issues a year, you can subscribe to △ (either print, online or through the △ App for iPad).

INSTITUTIONAL SUBSCRIPTION
£212/US$398 print or online

INSTITUTIONAL SUBSCRIPTION
£244/US$457 combined print & online

PERSONAL-RATE SUBSCRIPTION
£120/US$189 print and iPad access

STUDENT-RATE SUBSCRIPTION
£75/US$117 print only

To subscribe to print or online:
Tel: +44 (0) 1243 843 272
Email: cs-journals@wiley.com

△ APP FOR iPAD
For information on the △ App for iPad go to www.architectural-design-magazine.com
6-issue subscription: £44.99/US$64.99
Individual issue: £9.99/US$13.99

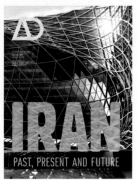

Volume 82 No 3
ISBN 978 1119 974505

Volume 82 No 4
ISBN 978 1119 973621

Volume 82 No 5
ISBN 978 1119 972662

Volume 82 No 6
ISBN 978 1118 336410

Volume 83 No 1
ISBN 978 1119 978657

Volume 83 No 2
ISBN 978 1119 952862

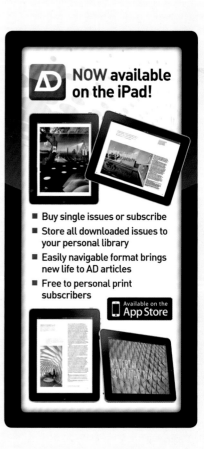

NOW available on the iPad!

- Buy single issues or subscribe
- Store all downloaded issues to your personal library
- Easily navigable format brings new life to AD articles
- Free to personal print subscribers

Available on the App Store